Made in Hong Kong

Love, Loss and the Long Way Home

An Adoptee's Search for Family and Belonging

Laura Tan

After decades of searching for her birth family, and after the famous UK TV programme Long Lost Family closed her case, 58 year old transracial adoptee Laura Tan decided to give it one last shot.

She booked the cheapest return flight to Hong Kong, a bunk in an eight bed dorm and gave herself 90 days to complete her quest, with a deadline of returning to the UK on Valentines Day.

A memoir that will break open your heart, make you laugh and cry, and that will stay with you long after you turn the last page.

Join Laura on a journey across decades and continents to an 'against all odds' ending you will never forget.

"*A brilliant writer with a very interesting story to tell.*"
Cathy Rentzenbrink, author of Sunday Times bestseller The Last Act of Love, A Manual for Heartache and Write It All Down

For Tom and Lucy Gibbs,
and for Phoebe and Chloe Gibbs.

May this book inspire and guide you,
just as you continue to inspire and guide me.

"The ultimate sacrifice a human can make. To give your child away to a stranger so that the child can have the chance (in life) that you could never have.

We only hope that the little girl had a chance to reinvent her life."

Alain Boublil (lyricist) and Claude-Michel Schönberg (composer)

Miss Saigon.

"They've got a wall in China
It's a thousand miles long
To keep out the foreigner
They made it strong
I've got a wall around me
You can't even see
It took a little time
To get to me"

— Paul Simon, *Something So Right*

TABLE OF CONTENTS

PROLOGUE

At ten weeks old, I started building a wall.

I didn't know I was doing it, of course. I had no words for the white-walled orphanage in Hong Kong, no language for the silence between feedings, or the cool wooden bars that defined my world. My only possession was a crumpled name tag—Yuk Lan—tied by a rubber band to the side of my cot, always just out of reach. There were no lullabies, no arms that lingered. Only routine.

By the time I was flown to England to join a British Christian family, the wall had taken shape. Not solid, exactly—more like mist layered over stone. Porous, but there. I didn't cry much. I smiled when I was supposed to.

Later, I learnt how to make it look like something else—achievement, gratitude, performance. I journalled about blessings. I said thank you.

The wall kept me safe. But it kept others out too. And over time, it grew heavy with things I hadn't named.

It wasn't a grand event that brought it down. No obvious tragedy. Just one bright afternoon in St Ives, in 2018. The kind of afternoon where the light dazzles off the harbour and the gulls sound unreasonably joyful.

I was 57, sitting cross-legged on an unmade bed in the top-floor flat we'd bought for the view—a place we thought would hold us together. Outside, the sea shifted its blues with the wind. Inside, something slipped. A crack, then a slow collapse. I didn't notice it at first. I thought I was just tired.

From the outside, things looked fine, enviable. We lived in the happiest town in Britain. I wore good clothes. Smiled for photos. But something had begun to fray—quietly, insistently—like thread pulled from the hem of a dress. The kind of thing you could miss, until you didn't.

Some days I retreated into silence. Other days, into my library of self-help books, or endless scrolling, cocooned in the worn softness of my red onesie. It wasn't always clear what had been said, only that something had passed between us—sharp, familiar, unresolved. The kind of exchange where no one raises their voice, but the air seems to vanish, just enough that it feels we forget how to breathe.

Later, standing in the shower, I tried to wash it off—the silence, the ache. I reached for the bottle marked *Inner Strength*, the one I always turned to when I needed anchoring. The scent—frankincense and clary sage—rose with the steam, familiar and steadying. I pressed it to my skin like a kind of prayer. A sliver of sea air slipped through the window. I breathed it in. I was still here.

I dressed carefully. Not to impress—more like a peace offering. A white shirt. Jeans. Something solid. Predictable. Adult. Not the red onesie—dismissed, more than once, as childish.

But the weight of something unsaid still pressed at the edge of the day.

And then, a memory arrived. A photograph. Faded at the edges. A little girl—five, maybe—standing on a tree stump in the garden of her first English home. Her back is to the camera, face tilted slightly, gazing at something far beyond the frame.

I hadn't thought of her in years. But there she was, suddenly, vividly. And I knew: she hadn't stopped searching. Neither had I.

Always searching. It had been said so many times before—sometimes as a joke, sometimes not. But this time, it landed as something else: not concern, but judgment. As if wanting to understand made me weak. As if introspection was something to be ashamed of.

But I knew then—the searching wasn't the problem. I searched. He didn't. That was all.

Yes, I have been searching. Still am. Maybe I always will be.

I would go to Hong Kong. Not to fix what was missing, but to follow what still called.

This journey—threaded through loss, silence, fragments of names and places—is far from over.

But maybe, just maybe, it's the act of searching that will lead me home.

INTRODUCTION

My name is Laura Tan. My Chinese name is Tang Yuk Lan. I was born in a hut in Hong Kong on 20th October 1960.

At 15 months old, in February 1962, I was sent to the UK to be adopted by a white British family—Catherine (Cath) and Arthur Enock, along with their two birth children, Christopher (6) and Ruth (4). They lived in a two-up, two-down terraced house in Leamington Spa.

I had spent ten weeks with my birth mother, So Kam Lai, before she placed me in Po Leung Kuk orphanage for temporary care while she was hospitalised. But she never returned. At six and a half months, she gave written consent for me to be adopted. The Director of Social Welfare in Hong Kong acted as my guardian while I was first "boarded out" and eventually adopted by the Enocks in November 1963, just after I turned three.

My adoption broke down in my teens. At 17, I nearly died from an accidental drug overdose. I was expelled from a private girls' school in the middle of my A-levels—despite having won a full scholarship. By the age of 20, I was estranged from my entire family. Cath, my adoptive mother, refused all contact and destroyed my adoption records—my passport, birth certificate, my birth mother's statement, and the few items I had brought from Hong Kong.

For years I tried to track down replacement records. In February 2002, exactly 40 years after I'd arrived in the UK, I finally uncovered a file that had been held all those years by Warwickshire County Council's Fostering and Adoption Unit. Armed with better information, I continued searching. Through my solicitor, I contacted both the Hong Kong Social Welfare Department (HKSWD) and the British Red Cross. Each said they couldn't help—and referred me to the other.

The searching continued, on and off. I had a young family, a business, a messy divorce—life got in the way. Then suddenly, I was in my fifties. It was as if someone had hit the fast-forward button, and the years had flickered by in a blur. I was married for a second time to my husband Martin, had two grown-up children, Tom and Lucy, a baby granddaughter, Phoebe, and—at last—some time on my hands.

Lucy wanted to know more about her heritage. About the grandmother she had never met. And I wanted to have answers ready for Phoebe, in case she ever asked questions of her own. I restarted the search, this time with new determination. I applied to the TV show *Long Lost Family*—not once, but twice. The first time, they rejected me outright, a swift "no." But I didn't give up. The second time, after weeks of calls, forms, interviews, and legal agreements, they finally took me on. I filled out paperwork, fielded questions, signed the contracts. For a whole year, they kept my hope alive: "We're on your case," they said. Each time I got an update, I let myself believe this might be it. That they were getting closer. That I was finally going to find the answers. Then, one day, came the email: they were stopping. Case shut. Little explanation. Just the same as before—hope snatched away, quietly, without warning.

So I decided to go myself.

Some friends thought I was mad when I told them I was flying to Hong Kong with barely any Cantonese, shaky Mandarin, and only scraps of information. But I'd never felt surer of anything. I needed to go. To return to the place I'd come from.

On November 14th, 2018, I boarded a plane to Hong Kong. My return flight was booked for Valentine's Day, 14th February 2019. Ninety days. One last try to find my family.

This is the story of that search. But it's also the story of what came before—the childhood that led me there. And what came after.

It's told in three parts, blending fable, memory, adoption records, letters, and extracts from the blog I kept during the search. And woven through it all are the questions I've been asked throughout my life:

What was it like, being adopted?

Do you think it's affected your life?

Why try to find your birth family when you already had a family here?

As a child, I was told I should be grateful. "Think of the ones who got left behind. They probably died." I didn't realise it at the time, but I wasn't grateful. And those comments—well-meaning but ignorant—planted confusion and self-doubt that grew like bindweed. Tangling, smothering.

By writing it all down, instead of endlessly circling it in my head, I hope we—me, as I write, and you, as you read—might get closer to understanding the long shadow of transracial adoption. And why it's okay, even necessary, for some adoptees not to feel grateful.

I also want to celebrate what it means to finally come home. Not to a country, a culture, or a family. But to yourself. To the you that lives beyond any name—given, adopted, married or legal. The self you come to know when you realise that survival is not enough. That you were always meant to thrive, not just survive.

This book is for anyone who has ever dreamed of finding something—or someone—lost. And for anyone who still believes, despite everything, that the search is worth it.

PART ONE:

BIRTH AND ADOPTION - FROM HONG KONG TO THE UK

Always Searching. Starting Off in the UK

Always searching.

More feeling than thought. A thread I hadn't yet followed to its end.

A truth I didn't want to admit—but couldn't quite shake. I have spent my whole life sifting through records, faces, half-formed memories. Not always knowing what I was looking for—only that I needed to find something that would help the pieces of my story come together.

I remember the moment the search began. It started with a box. Old, battered, high on top of my parents' wardrobe. My adoption records.

My adopted siblings, Chris and Ruth, couldn't have cared less about the old box we found on top of our parents' wardrobe. They were more drawn to a newer one, full of little packets of condoms, bought in bulk for my adoptive dad, Arthur, to take into Fords Foundry, where he worked as a foreman, shop steward, and union rep. The condoms were one of many things bought in bulk for the Ford workers, my dad eager to help everybody save money on their 'something for the weekend'. That was the kind of man Arthur was—always ready to support others, even when it was a struggle for him.

Though he left school at fourteen and found writing difficult, Arthur was tireless in helping others. We had a steady stream of visitors to our door, seeking his advice. Sometimes quite late at night, after a full day's manual work, I'd watch him with pride as he marked lined scrap paper with the tip of his pencil, labouring over every word. He'd then transform his drafts into proper inked notes on crisp Basildon Bond stationery, determined to assist those needing help to challenge disciplinary actions or fight unfair dismissals.

I admired my dad. I liked how kind he was and I wanted to help others, be like him. But something inside me kept wondering… what if I had a different dad, another family somewhere? When I found the box of records, it was like a voice in my head got louder, asking questions I didn't know how to answer. Big questions that made my head hurt and my stomach ache.

Arthur made me feel safe. But with my adoptive mum, Cath, it was different. She gave me a home, but something was missing. I longed for her to love me more, to be proud of me. Even as a child, I sensed I wasn't the kind of daughter she had hoped for. I didn't need her in the way she wanted to be needed. I felt I had to earn her affection, to stay subdued, not shine too brightly against the backdrop of her expectations. As I blossomed, exceeded, and excelled, that uneasy balance began to unravel, revealing tensions beneath the surface.

Cath was a mature student, training to be a primary school teacher. Her homework sometimes involved her and her fellow students using me as a case study. I never struggled with the tasks they set me. When they praised my high test scores, I'd feel a warm glow, like the child in the Ready Brek advert. These, and my other 'good girl' memories, are fond ones.

At six, I was given the role of narrator in the school nativity play—perhaps because I was one of the few children who could read. Mrs Houghton smiled warmly as I read the first lines. My mum, skilled at transforming fabric remnants into dresses, had made me a red taffeta party dress with a net underskirt and huge sash bow. I felt so special as I climbed onto the podium. The room fell silent, and I heard someone gasp, "Oh, isn't she cute?" I was often the centre of attention—and I loved it.

At other times, I instinctively knew that blending in was key to making friends. I joined in wherever I could—country dancing with my classmates, carefully plaiting and unplaiting the red, white, and blue ribbons on our maypole. During PE lessons, I was chosen to play wing attack on the netball team, my plastic lanyard slipping constantly off my tiny shoulders as I darted around the court. On sports day, I ran in relay races, clutching the baton with determination, my heart pounding with the fear of dropping it and letting my team down. I wasn't always the fastest or the most coordinated, but I tried my best to be part of something—to belong.

Although I tried hard to be a good sport, blending in was tough. My heavy pink NHS glasses and braces marked me as different, as did the ease with which I excelled in English and Maths. It was remarkable, considering I had spent the first 15 months of my life in an orphanage in another country. I wore my weaknesses like a badge, hoping my friends would see that I, too, had hard days. When I tried to knit, I thought each dropped stitch might help me feel more normal—but every mistake felt like failure.

My mum's reactions made it harder. When I dropped a stitch, she'd yank the piece from my needles, unravel everything, and make me start over. I just wanted to be accepted and loved, but trying so hard only made me feel more alone. Instead of something beautiful, I ended up with a messy jumble, caught between wanting to fit in and wishing my mum could accept me as I was.

Crying was not an option; tears only brought harsher reprimands. I remember once crying out when she brushed my hair too roughly. She yanked it into a ponytail and, with sharp scissors, lopped off the gathered hair. "That'll teach you," she snapped.

In contrast, there was Mrs Smith, the kind school dinner lady who patiently helped me retrieve dropped stitches in my knitting endeavours. She guided me through my first completed project: a red woollen slot scarf with pointed ends, teaching me to rib knit and shape stitches. While many early craft attempts were tossed aside, I became a competent knitter and sewer. My first "outfit"—a pale pink, unevenly hemmed skirt with a matching bolero, trimmed in green Ric Rac—brought mixed emotions. I felt proud for making something of my own, but also ashamed of how it compared to the shop-bought clothes my friends wore. That sense of pride reminded me of how I'd felt wearing the red taffeta dress my mum made for me. It wasn't really about the clothes—it was about the care and attention stitched into them, even if her love for me felt conditional or absent in other ways. Maybe, in those moments, she was showing love in the only way she knew how.

Learning to ride a bike felt similar. My first proper bicycle was the best gift I'd ever received. It wasn't a hand-me-down. That Christmas, it sat in the hallway, mummified in brown paper, glittery blue paintwork peeking through. It felt like it had been preserved just for me.

But riding it was another matter. I fell endlessly, my knees constantly scabbed. My family, all skilled cyclists, ran rings around me. Still, I got back on. Eventually, I managed to ride up and down our street without falling. That small victory—like finishing the outfit—was enough for now.

Being on my bike, though wobbly at first, gave me a new sense of freedom. It also helped me make a couple of friends on our street. Yet I was always on the fringes—on the outside looking in. When there were no friends around, I turned to our many pets.

Our house was a menagerie. Mice, hamsters, rats, gerbils, a guinea pig. A budgie named Alice. A stray cat we called Apple because she nested on trays of apples from the allotment. Skinny Apple gave birth on a bed of Bramleys. There was Didiabolo, the huge black hare—another stray—who tried to bash into our rabbit Tenzing's hutch, as if he too were searching for somewhere to belong. Like me.

All of them were presided over by my mum, whose instinct was always to rescue. After seeing Bill Sikes' dog in *Oliver!*, my parents fell for English Bull Terriers. They bought a fawn bitch and named her Floss, hoping to breed and show her puppies. Floss had a litter of three. We kept Fred, an all-white bullie with a pirate-like black patch over one eye. His other eye, rimmed pink, gave him a permanently surprised look.

I claimed Fred as mine, even though he belonged to all of us. It was a childlike insistence, a need to have someone—something—to call my own. At the end of our garden, I'd teeter on stilts my dad had made, Fred balancing beside me on his hind legs. Together, we'd peer over the fence at the Grand Union Canal—me waving at passing barges, Fred yapping in delight. The sailors often waved back, unfazed by his strange looks.

We must've looked an odd pair—me, a small, wobbly Chinese girl with shiny black hair, and Fred, the egg-headed bullie with his pirate eye. But we didn't care. We were misfits, happy in our world.

Then, one day, Fred bit my mum. It seemed to come from nowhere. Her arm, bandaged thickly, hid stitches she said "went on forever."

"He has to go," she said. "Next time, it could be a child."

I froze. He was my Fred. That evening, he was taken to the vet. The next day, the garden was silent. I kept looking for him.

I don't remember if I cried when I hugged him goodbye. But I do remember staying silent. My throat tight. I remembered how Cath teased him—provoked him, just as she teased me. Fred hated shiny wrappers. I'd watched her wave one in his face, her fingers dancing, a gleam in her eye. He growled low. She didn't stop.

It was the same relentless teasing that left me in tears, or worse. Once, she tickled me behind the knees until I writhed away, slamming into the sharp corner of a three-bar electric fire. I ended up in Casualty, needing stitches near my eye. Fred wasn't like me—he didn't cry, didn't plead. He snapped. And he paid for it.

I learned early that people and animals respond differently under pressure. Some retreat, some endure, some fight back. I had learned to shrink myself, to mask pain with a smile, to stay silent when something hurt. Fred had lashed out—and it cost him everything. That contrast stayed with me. It showed me that survival could look very different depending on who you were, and what you had the power—or permission—to express.

When I was nearly nine, my brother accidentally slammed a plate glass door on me—fed up with my constant coming and going and the relentless knocking to be let back in. I fell straight through it, shards of glass flying, blood everywhere. A neighbour rushed me to hospital, my wrist wrapped hastily in tea towels, red seeping through like ink. I needed seven stitches and was left with a jagged scar that still shows today. It had narrowly missed an artery.

But it wasn't the blood or the pain that lingered most. It was my mum's reaction. Sharp, impatient, almost annoyed. When she arrived at the hospital, there was no softness, no comfort—just scolding. That same night, she insisted we still go to the showing of *Paint Your Wagon* at the local cinema. So I put on my bravest, happiest face, even though I was tired and everything felt muddled inside my head. I managed the first half, but then I fell asleep, numb from more than just exhaustion.

That day reinforced what I was already beginning to understand: in our house, pain, confusion—even identity—were things to be ignored or denied. My origins were never spoken of. My feelings were inconvenient. So I learned to negate them too, becoming complicit in the silence. I masked discomfort, performed normality, smiled when everything inside me ached. I laughed when I wanted to cry. I stayed silent when I longed to scream.

Keeping us children and animals fed and protected must have been a challenge for my parents. They were always on a tight budget, yet somehow managed to nourish us and keep us mostly safe. I often think about how much better my education was compared to what I might have received if I'd stayed in the orphanage. My primary school days were filled with exciting after-school activities—Brownies, ballet, piano lessons. My parents scrimped and saved to enhance our lives and prospects, and I find comfort in those happier memories.

One that stands out is the brand-new burgundy Ford Escort Estate my dad bought at a discount through his job at Ford's Foundry. To house it, he built a garage, brick by brick, out there in all weathers after a long day at the factory. I'd watch him in the dusk, whistling as he worked, mixing sand and cement, cutting bricks, determined to finish what he started. He couldn't drive, so it was my mum behind the wheel, with the rest of us crammed in around her, heading off on family outings.

We were proud—ours was the first new car on the street. I remember being squashed in the boot space with Fred, while Chris and Ruth nestled beside Floss in the back seat. Our annual camping trip to St David's in Wales was the highlight of our summer. My dad would fit a roof rack and hitch up the trailer for our heavy blue canvas tent with its two yellow sleeping compartments. "Don't touch the sides," was our parents' mantra—because if you did, the rain would seep in.

On the surface, those years looked blissful, filled with new adventures and the pride of building a life together—like the garage, the camping trailer, the memories stitched into every picnic and soggy tent corner. There were camping holidays, animals galore, cheerful outings in our shiny new car. There was laughter, structure, even joy. But beneath that surface was a strange, persistent ache. An emptiness I couldn't quite name. I belonged, and yet I didn't. I was held, but not fully seen. I was loved, perhaps—but not always for who I really was.

Even in moments of happiness, I felt that quiet tension—like a wire pulled taut inside me. I couldn't articulate it then, but something deep down kept whispering: you don't quite fit. Not here. Not yet. And that's when we found that box. Chris and Ruth were disinterested but I sensed those papers were significant. I knew better than to flaunt them in front of my family. Later, when I was alone, I used a broom handle to knock the forbidden box off the top of the wardrobe. As a competent reader, even at a young age, I secretly read what I could manage in one short sitting, trying to piece together my story from faded documents that spoke of another life – a life I was curious about but didn't fully understand. The following day, at school, I boasted to anyone who would listen, that I had been born in a hut in Hong Kong and had a few weeks with a foster family before coming to live with my new family in

Leamington Spa. Being so young, I didn't fully grasp the significance or value of my find. The records were intact then and it wasn't until much later, at age 40, when I tried to retrieve them, that I realised they were gone.

In all the 19 years I spent with my adoptive family, nobody ever talked about my adoption or my Chinese heritage. Maybe they mentioned it when I was little, laughing about how I struggled to pronounce my name, turning 'Laura Enock' into 'LawlaEnock.' They would repeat it, doubled over in laughter, enjoying their favourite stories about me as a four-year-old. I remember proudly pointing at a big white bird and exclaiming, "Look, that swan's got wings on!". I wanted my mum to see how brave I was for getting close enough to notice the rings on the swan's legs. Instead, she burst out laughing, and they all joined in, finding joy in my speech impediment, as if it were a punchline to a joke. I ricocheted from being the centre of attention as an exemplary pupil to suffering as an object of ridicule and curiosity. School friends and even strangers on the street were always asking where I was from and why my family didn't look like me. I quickly learned that no more than two sentences were needed to satisfy their curiosity and bring the conversation to a halt: "I'm from Hong Kong," and "I was adopted." This way, I could avoid more questions I didn't know how to answer.

As a teenager and young adult, I tried hard not to get riled by ill-conceived assumptions. "Oh, so your parents own that Ming Kee takeaway," or "You must be here to study" or "You must be a Nurse at the Warneford Hospital." Once a friend mentioned seeing a photograph of me in our local art gallery. I had been captured unaware in front of a statue of Queen Victoria. I went to see for myself. The black and white poster showcased me wearing my favourite Afghan coat, flared corduroy jeans and cheesecloth wrap shirt. My windswept and tousled hair added to the artistic and flattering nature of the photograph that should have delighted me, except that it did not. For it was labelled "TOURIST."

So much of my identity was slipping away, and I was overwhelmed by confusion about an identity I had yet to fully understand. Even my surname Enock added to the confusion. Adults would often correct the spelling of my name, misled by biblical and political influences. Enoch Powell frequently made headlines and appeared on TV for his extreme anti-immigration views and his famous Rivers of Blood speech. Similarly, Robert Relf, who lived on my street had been on TV for placing a 'For Sale, but not to coloured people' sign in his front garden. I knew for certain how to spell my surname, but I was never entirely sure whether I was truly welcome in my new home and country.

It's no wonder, then, that I was uncertain who I really was and felt an urgent need to understand myself better—and to discover where in the world I might truly belong. Yet I couldn't help but feel guilty whenever I asked for more information.

That teasing and ridiculing of my Chinese identity by my family when I was a child later developed into something far more destructive and hurtful. When I was 19, things came to a head. My relationship with my adoptive mother had always been fragile, but that year it shattered completely. I remember how painful those weeks were—of being sent to Coventry, of walking into a room and being met with silence. If I stood up to her, I was slapped. If I tried to explain myself, I was ignored. The tension hung heavy in the house, thick and unspoken. I was made to feel unwelcome in my own home, and slowly it became unbearable. One day, after yet another argument about the suitability of my boyfriend, I packed a few belongings and walked out. I left behind not only my childhood home, but the illusion that I had ever truly belonged there. I moved in with my boyfriend, whose family had taken me under their wing.

They showered me with kindness and care that felt like a healing salve. The Batty family welcomed me without question. Their name alone felt like a funny gift, adding a layer of humour to the tenderness they offered me. Jim's mother cooked my favourite meals—stew and dumplings and roast dinner—and introduced me to their Friday night ritual of Chinese takeaway, something that felt both ironic and comforting. She offered to help me alter my clothes, and sometimes, she'd quietly take my work uniform and return it washed and ironed—the small but thoughtful gestures of someone who saw me and cared. It wasn't just the things Jim's mother did for me I hadn't known before—the meals and the laundry—it was the way she hugged me and smiled at me whenever I arrived, the gentle way she spoke to me as if it were the most natural thing in the world. I was unprepared for the simplicity of his family's kindness. It chipped away at the walls I hadn't realised I had built to protect myself against my own family, each small gesture a reminder of what I had been missing—a reminder that there were places where I could be cared for and loved.

Returning home to visit my own family one day, I was met with a wall of silence and refused entry to my childhood home. My adoptive mother had made her decision, and the rest of the family fell into line. Nobody questioned her. Nobody stood up for me. I was cast out, not just by her, but by all of them—either too afraid or too complicit to intervene. The suddenness and severity of the rejection felt orchestrated, deliberate. My attempts to reach out, to repair our fractured relationship, were met with silence. The door was shut in my face, the phone was hung up, and letters went unanswered. Her silence became theirs. It was as though I had never been part of the family at all.

Much later, when I had almost resigned myself to never having further contact with the Enocks, everything changed with the birth of my son, Tom. The days following his arrival had been perfect—until they weren't. Just as we were about to be discharged, a nurse noticed how jaundiced he was while I was learning to bathe him. I had thought his yellowness was just a trait from his Chinese heritage, but this was the first time a professional had seen him undressed. My naïveté became painfully clear. Tom was rushed to the special care baby unit, and I ended up staying in the hospital for another week as he underwent blood transfusions to prevent brain damage. A recently qualified paediatrician, who had encountered a similar case in Hong Kong, determined that Tom was suffering from G6PDD, an enzyme deficiency causing his severe jaundice.

The stress and worry left me physically and emotionally drained. But after Tom had pulled through, exhaustion finally overtook me, and I allowed myself to sleep. When I woke, I was startled to see my dad standing at the foot of my bed, holding a huge bunch of yellow roses. At first, I thought I was still dreaming. I hadn't told him about Tom or my extended stay—my husband must have contacted him.

The yellow roses were such a simple gesture, but they carried enormous significance after years of silence, especially knowing that my dad would never normally splash out on shop-bought flowers. He was more likely to hand over a string-tied bunch of dahlias from his allotment. This was the turning point in our relationship. Tom made a full recovery, and I left the hospital with my newborn son, clutching my dad's roses, filled with hope for all our futures.

Slowly but surely, dad and I stitched together the frayed edges of our relationship, mending what had once seemed beyond repair. After Tom was born, we began to reconnect. Dad, having grown tired of being controlled by mum's expectations, seemed more relaxed and more present. He started popping in for tea, sharing conversations, and eventually spending time with both Tom and Lucy. Over the years, he became a part of our lives again—not just a visitor, but family.

One day, as I watched Lucy filling in her homework sheet, "My Family Tree," it struck me how much of my own history was still a mystery. Her tree had gaping holes where the names of her maternal family should have been. She knew Arthur was her grandfather, but there were entire branches missing, parts of my past she didn't know—whether by birth or adoption, the gaps loomed large.

It was my dad I turned to, to try and help me. I was approaching 40, yet still frightened of rocking the boat.

"Dad, I know it's been years, but I really want to know…" I began, my voice small and apologetic, fearing that I might push too hard and unravel the tentative peace we had finally found. "Do you think you could retrieve my adoption records and belongings for me?"

My dad said he'd try, but nothing materialised, even after a few gentle reminders.

A year later I broached the subject again. "I think Cath threw it all away," he sheepishly admitted, clearly hoping I wouldn't bring it up again.

What I was asking for wasn't much. I simply wanted to know what had happened to the few belongings that had come with me from Hong Kong. The small teal and white BOAC (British Overseas Airways Corporation) bag I last saw when its handles were coming unstitched and the bag itself was fraying and growing mouldy. Where was the one toy I had brought with me from Hong Kong? The small inflatable Father Christmas that had developed a hole at the seam where the white bobble connected to his red hat, rendering him useless despite my childish attempts to mend it with tape. What had become of the clothes I wore upon arrival? The white fluffy coat and hat with its dangling pom poms. I thought about my baby passport and identification bracelet. All my belongings had vanished. That box of paperwork I had discovered on top of my parents' wardrobe. Where had it all gone?

The only other proper conversation I ever had with my dad regarding my adoption was when I inquired about my birth mother. "I think they (Hong Kong Social Services) tried to find her," he replied. "But she was dead." At the age of 58, after my adoptive dad had died, I discovered that his initial statement had been true. Hong Kong Social Services had indeed attempted to locate her. However, the second part, the claim of her death—well, that turned out to be a lie.

I had hoped that having my dad back in my life would fill the gaps in my identity. But as Jeanette Winterson writes in *Why Be Happy When You Could Be Normal?*, being adopted is like having the first chapters of your life torn out of the book. This metaphor resonated with me as I grew older, realising that our identities are woven from many strands: the people we love, the families we choose or are chosen by, and the stories written about us long before we could tell them ourselves. For me, those stories lay scattered across fragile, now-lost documents—echoes of a history I had never fully known. I needed to find those pieces and understand the truth of who I really was.

My Seven Names

Before I settled on the title Made in Hong Kong, I considered calling this memoir Seven Names, because I've had that many. Each one a thread, woven into the strange, beautiful, and often unravelled fabric of my life.

Having seven names has caused complications. That fabric is tattered and worn. In 2022, after a long application process, I finally secured a mortgage offer—only to discover it had accidentally been issued under a name that included my long-discarded middle name, Gillian. When a sharp-eyed legal professional spotted the discrepancy, the offer was withdrawn. I had to reapply, during the chaos of the Truss/Kwarteng mini-budget, when mortgage lenders were pulling products and interest rates were soaring. I got a new offer, but at a higher rate. The dent in my wallet I can handle. It's the repeated dent in my identity that still stings. Especially when it strikes at my heritage.

My first attempt to get a Chinese visa was in 2010. I was driving an ambulance from England to Mongolia on a charity rally. After leaving the ambulance in Mongolia, I planned to catch a train from Mongolia into mainland China and return back home from there. But my visa application was refused. Then in 2014, I applied three more times, wanting to join Martin on a business trip to China. Twice, I applied by post through an agency that claimed they could "get a Chinese visa fast." But a woman with seven names, apparently, is not fast-tracked. Both postal applications were rejected. So I went in person to the Chinese Embassy. I thought: if they saw my Chinese face, if they recognised me as one of their own, I'd be accepted.

No.

The embassy official didn't even look up. He struck a thick red line through my application. "Too many names. You don't have Hong Kong ID in name you got now. No visa."

That same day, Martin was granted a two-year business visa.

There's a particular kind of shame that comes from not being recognised by your own people. Money lost on a mortgage deal is nothing compared with the pain of being turned away—not for what you've done, but for who you are. Or who you think you are. Because when you've had seven names and no clear lineage, even your identity feels like guesswork. You carry pieces of memory, pieces of paper, fragments of a story—none of which are enough. You're left outside a door that should open, holding a version of yourself you can't quite prove.

I digress. I started this chapter to talk about the names.

As a child, when asked what I wanted to be when I grew up, I lied. I'd say a brain surgeon. Or, if I was feeling brave, a dolphin tamer. But the truth? I wanted to be a writer. I devoured Enid Blyton books under my candlewick bedspread, torch hidden under my pillow. I was told never to name her as my favourite author—especially not at my scholarship interview for the prestigious Kings High School for Girls. I must've held my tongue, because I was accepted as a non-fee paying pupil.

On my first day at Kings High, my dad hugged me at the bus stop, brushing cat hair off my black blazer. He straightened the strap of the oversized leather satchel we'd chosen together—an expensive purchase for a man who handed over every week's wages to his wife in a brown envelope. He stood on the kerb, waving long and hard as the bus pulled away. As if I were returning to Hong Kong, not just going to the next town.

Only now do I see what I might have meant to him. An atonement. A daughter born of the place where he once fought. My dad was a Korean war veteran. In his early twenties, he'd been stationed in Hong Kong and fought in Korea against Chinese forces. He never spoke of it to me. I only discovered the details of his service when his former Sergeant

Major shared them at his funeral in 2014. No wonder he never said much. And no wonder it felt important to him that we kept up appearances. A silent peace offering from a soldier carrying private ghosts.

My mother, Cath, was ecstatic I'd got into such a prestigious school. But her pride felt skewed—more like victory than joy. She'd fought to adopt me. Fought with Warwickshire County Council and Hong Kong Social Services to get the adoption finalised. Fought for the tax credit for a third child. Fought to get me into that school.

Cath always fought—often on my behalf. But as I got older, her battles weren't just with officials and institutions—they were with *me*. She taught me how to challenge rules, how to push back against authority. And then, somewhere along the way, I became *her* opponent.

At sixteen, still her student but no longer her disciple, I tried on her fighting spirit like a coat two sizes too big. I wore my skirt too short, my heels too high, swapped my regulation V-neck for a hand-knit jumper. During the general election, I marched into school with a stack of Labour posters Cath had sent me in with and plastered them defiantly across the noticeboard—a slash of red in a sea of Conservative blue. They stood out like I did, bold, awkward, impossible to ignore.

Once, in response to an English essay titled "Now for something really interesting," I handed in a piece called *It's All About Me*, expecting scorn. But Mrs Hall returned my homework with a huge grin. She'd marked it with a big red A-. "You write interestingly about yourself," she wrote. "I'd like to hear more."

That comment stayed with me. So here I am, Mrs Hall. Telling more. Starting with the seven names.

THE SAID INFANT (1960)

In all early Hong Kong Social Welfare documents, I was not given a name—only referred to as *"The Said Infant."* A phrase that sounded more like evidence than a person.

TANG YUK LAN (1961)

My Chinese name. In Chinese tradition, the family name comes first—so "Tang" was my surname, though it wasn't my father's. It was the name of the man my mother lived with. She added it to my birth certificate when I was already six months old and in the orphanage—perhaps as a legal formality, or out of desperation. According to her later statement, she was starving, destitute, and living with him when I was born. "Yuk Lan" was my given name—jade orchid, magnolia, beautiful flower. Years later, I would misremember it as Tan Yuk Lang. After my divorce, I changed my name by deed poll to Laura Tan—when it should have been Laura Tang.

PENNY (1962)

Given by my British foster family, the Starkeys, before I was adopted. I'd always believed I'd lived in foster care, but only in 2019—when I accessed my records from the National Children's Home (now Action for Children)—did I find written confirmation.

"Penny" doesn't appear on any official documents, but I remember my adoptive parents telling me I once had this name. Babies were often placed with British families in Hong Kong to ease the transition from orphanage to overseas adoption—and to help them gain weight, as many were undernourished.

I was likely with the Starkeys only briefly.

I've sometimes (unkindly) thought of that time as *"fattening the calf."*

LAURA GILLIAN ENOCK (1962–1983)

The name given by my adoptive parents. They never used "Penny," and keeping any part of my Chinese name was never considered.

LAURA GILLIAN GIBBS (1985–1996)

My first married name. I took it with relief—escaping the name Enock and everything it carried. The wedding was small, at Warwick Registry Office on a snowy Saturday in April 1985. Not one of my adopted family

RSVP'd to the invitation I sent. I secretly hoped they might turn up and surprise me. They didn't. The first person who spoke to me that morning was the Registrar's assistant, who asked if I needed a translator. To this day I wonder how she would have reacted if I had said yes.

LAURA PEMBERTON (2000)

Briefly adopted after my second marriage to Martin. But there were already too many Mrs Pembertons in his life—his ex-wife, his sister, his mother. I tired of hearing my name called and not recognising it. Once, in an optician's waiting room, they called "Mrs Pemberton" three times before I realised it was me. The name never quite felt like mine.

LAURA TAN (1996–now)

A name I chose. At the time, I had no birth records—only a memory: *Tan Yuk Lang*. Later I learned it had been *Tang Yuk Lan*, but I'm glad I got it wrong. "Tang" was the name of the man who left my mother. Not one I'd be proud to carry.

If I'd known her story then—her name, her sorrow—I might have chosen *Laura Wong*, or *Laura Lai*, in her honour.

But another name? I'm done with that.

Birth Mother's Statement

I found my birth records in a cardboard box discarded on top of my adoptive parents' wardrobe. I was around eight, and though I couldn't understand the full weight of the documents at the time, one stood out even then—my birth mother's statement. As a child, I had no idea how significant that paper would become. Years later, I was left reeling when I discovered my adoptive mother had thrown away everything connected to the beginning of my life—not just the paperwork, but the physical traces of who I was before I arrived in England. It felt like an erasure, a stripping away of identity. Perhaps she did it in anger, disappointed that I had not become the helpless, dutiful daughter she had hoped for.

The search to recover those lost records was long and disheartening. I contacted several organisations, including NORCAP—the National Organisation for the Reunification of Adopted Children and Parents—but got nowhere. For years, I felt like I was chasing ghosts. Then, by sheer coincidence, while working at Warwickshire County Council, and in my early forties, I overheard colleagues from the Education of Traveller and Refugee Children team discussing the department responsible for fostering and adoption.

It was a light bulb moment. I'd spent so long looking outward, and here they were, people who could help me—right where I worked.

I contacted the fostering and adoption unit. There had been a recent fire; many files were lost. For a week I waited, not knowing. Then Jill, a social worker, called. My file had survived. We arranged to meet.

That grey February afternoon, while a friend looked after Tom and Lucy, I sat with Jill in a small office, bracing myself. She had read my file carefully and had summarised key dates in her notes. She was warm, respectful, and thorough. She knew I had already had extensive therapy, trained as a therapist myself, and was now working for the Educational

Psychology team. So she kept the obligatory counselling brief, and we got to the moment I had dreamed of for decades: the opening of the file.

Among the redacted lines and formal statements, I found what I had longed to see—that document I'd glimpsed as a child. My birth mother's statement, dated 2nd May 1961.

When she made her declaration, I was six and a half months old and had already spent four months in Po Leung Kuk. In her statement, my mother gave up custody of me—TANG Yuk Lan, "the said infant"—to the Director of Social Welfare. She granted him the right to pass me on to whomever he saw fit.

Is it any wonder I sometimes feel like a relay baton—dropped, passed on, picked up again, passed on once more?

Here is the full text of her statement:

"I, LAI So-Kam (Chinese characters for her name), Identity Card No. 147628, residing at an unnumbered hut inside the Melon Garden, Kam Shan Village, Tai Po, New Territories (Chinese characters for address), do solemnly, sincerely and truly declare as follows.

I am a widow (my late husband WONG Kam-Kee's death certificate No. 37/58 Tai Po refers).

After my husband's death on 17.3.58, I co-habited with one WONG Tin (Chinese characters for name) whose wife was then in Mainland China. When I was about to give birth to an infant, the wife of WONG Tin came to Hong Kong with their children and I had to stay away from him. Owing to financial difficulties, I again cohabited with another man TANG Kam-wah (Chinese characters for name) otherwise known as TANG Tin (Chinese characters for name) on the very day of the infant's birth.

On the 20th day of October 1960, I gave birth to a female infant TANG Yuk-Lan (Chinese characters for name) at the home of TANG Tin at hut, Hung Shui Kiu, New Territories. The birth of the said female infant was registered at the Births & Deaths Registry on the 21st day of

February 1961 (Birth Certificate No. 48 P.R. Pin Shan). Since I had already left the natural father, WONG Tin, I put the name TANG Kam-wah in the birth certificate as the father of the said infant. I refer to a copy of the said Birth Certificate upon which marked with a letter "A", I have endorsed my name prior to completing this declaration.

In December 1960, I was suffering from kidney disease (Nephrosis) and was sent to Pok Oi Hospital, Un Long (Chinese characters for hospital) for medical treatment. At the same time, the said infant was recommended to enter Po Leung Kuk for temporary care by the District Officer, Un Long on 31st December 1960.

TANG Kam-wah left me after my hospitalisation and I have to take care of my four children single-handed. Since I am really not in a position to look after the said infant, TANG Yuk-Lan, who is still in Po Leung Kuk, I have agreed to part with and have parted with the custody of the said infant to the Director of Social Welfare, Causeway Bay Magistracy Building, Hong Kong, to the intent that the Director of Social Welfare may retain the custody and control of the said infant. And that he may hand over the custody and control of the said infant to whomsoever he considers suitable and may permit the said infant to be removed from the Colony, or that when an application for an adoption order is made in respect of the said infant, this may serve as my consent.

I understand that the nature and effect of the handing over of the said infant to the Director of Social Welfare or of an adoption order is to deprive a parent or guardian of all parental rights in respect of the maintenance and upbringing of the said infant, and I hereby renounce forever all claims on the said infant. I have neither given nor received nor been promised any financial or other consideration to or by or on behalf of the Director of Social Welfare with relation to the handing over of the care and custody of the said infant to him."

Statutory Declaration made by my birth mother, LAI So-Kam. No signature—just a cross and left thumb print. She was illiterate.

Declared and signed at the Social Welfare Department, Hong Kong on 2nd May 1961 before A.T.R. Jackson, Justice of the Peace.

The English document was signed by Social Welfare Officer LO Shu-Wing, who acted as interpreter.

Reading it again now, I can feel her desperation, her sorrow stitched into every formal phrase. No signature—just a thumbprint—but I hear her voice between the lines. She gave me up so I could have a future. And this document, cold as it seems, is the closest I've ever come to hearing her say goodbye.

Getting to Grips with Adoption. Why? How?

Getting to Grips with Adoption. Why? How? As I continue with my memoir and try to answer questions that have lingered, it seems that understanding the intricacies of adoption might be helpful for unravelling my life story. Not only is it an opportunity for me to confront the buried confusion, sadness and anger that shaped me, but it might also provide insight to readers who've stumbled upon this memoir.

Discussing my adoption was always a precarious endeavour. I've been asked countless questions over the years—about being adopted, about why I went searching, and about how I became estranged from my adoptive family. For a long time, I dismissed enquiries about my past, afraid of the emotions that would resurface if I dared to peel back the layers of my story. Now, I'm willing to delve in. To make it feel safer, I've chosen to tackle the questions in a methodical, structured way. Doing so creates a protective frame—like filling in a questionnaire rather than writing a confession. It lets me step back just enough to explore my early years with a clearer head. At the same time, I hope it explains why going in search of my birth family became so important.

The first question I'm often asked is: Why were you adopted?

When people ask this, they're usually trying to understand why my parents chose adoption. But this seemingly simple question hides more beneath the surface. I think it breaks down into three parts:

a) What motivated my parents to adopt? What was their backstory? b) Why me? Was I specifically chosen? c) How did an English couple in the early 1960s end up adopting a Chinese baby?

a) Why did they adopt? The reasons behind my parents' decision to adopt have always been a bit of a mystery. They already had two biological children, a boy and a girl. From what I've gathered, complications during Cath's second pregnancy (Rhesus incompatibility) meant doctors advised against having another child. So, out of either selfless compassion or a desire to soothe something unresolved within herself, Cath and my father adopted me. I'll never know their full motivations. But I hope that, in those early days, I brought my mother some comfort amidst her own uncertainties.

b) Why did they adopt me? As for why they adopted *me* specifically—well, it turns out I wasn't the child they were originally expecting. They had anticipated the arrival of another baby girl, only to be told, at the last minute, that she couldn't travel from Hong Kong due to health concerns. Disappointed but determined, my mother pleaded for a replacement. Yes—*a replacement baby.*

My parents likely went through some kind of vetting process. The local Methodist church served as a referee, and after I arrived, we continued attending services there. I was christened as a Methodist and went to Sunday school for about a year—until, quietly and without explanation, we stopped going.

These days, anyone wanting to adopt overseas must pay an application fee of £1,975 just to begin the process. Once matched to a child, they're required to visit the child's country of origin and confirm in writing that they wish to proceed.

My parents did none of these things. It seems I was simply put on a plane with an identity bracelet and a small British Overseas Airways Corporation (BOAC) bag, chaperoned by a flight attendant. The flight from Hong Kong in 1962 would have taken nearly 24 hours—almost double the time it takes today. Planes couldn't fly over Russia then, adding hours to the journey.

My adoptive family picked me up from the flight attendant at Heathrow Airport. But there was no "click" in "click and collect." No choosing. Just collect. I imagine myself a little like Paddington Bear. I had my name tag, my bag, and—while I wasn't carrying a marmalade sandwich—if someone had tied a note around my neck reading *"please look after this baby,"* it wouldn't have felt far from the truth.

All my life I have yearned to feel special. To be *the chosen one*. But sometimes, my beginning feels more like a random (un)lucky dip.

c) **How did a white British couple in the 1960s come to adopt a Chinese baby?** To answer this, you need a little historical context. Fans of *Call the Midwife* might recall the storyline about May Tang, a Hong Kong adoptee. It wasn't just creative writing—there was real history behind it.

In the aftermath of Mao's Great Leap Forward, famine and political upheaval pushed thousands across the border into Hong Kong. Refugee families crowded into makeshift camps. Many could not feed another mouth. Babies—especially girls—were abandoned daily.

In response, international agencies stepped in. The UN had declared 1959–1960 the "World Refugee Year," drawing global attention to crises like Hong Kong's. International Social Services (ISS) began coordinating overseas adoptions, placing babies in the U.S., Canada, and the UK.

Between 1958 and 1965, more than 770 babies left Hong Kong this way. I was one of them.

I didn't know any of this. I didn't even know there *were* others. Then, at 49, out of the blue, I received a request from BAAF (British Association for Adoption and Fostering) asking me to participate in a research project about all the babies that had been adopted to the UK from Hong Kong in the 1960s. All the babies? So my adoption had been part of a carefully orchestrated programme. I wasn't alone. Somewhere out there were other women like me, with similar beginnings.

I was part of something bigger. A project. A programme. And yet, my parents had never told me. Just like so much else, it had been kept quiet.

My adoptive mother had simply answered a national appeal. She couldn't have known how her choice would shape the course of my life. But it did. Profoundly.

Getting to Grips with Adoption. What Was It Like?

If the first question is *"why?"*—the second is always *"what was it like?"* It's a reasonable question. People are often curious about what adoption *feels* like from the inside.

The truth is: it's complex. From my earliest memories of feeling like an outsider in my adoptive family, to my lifelong longing for a connection with my birth roots, themes of identity, sadness, and belonging thread through the story. Sometimes they knot. Sometimes they fray.

I once typed "adoption" into Google. It returned 2.6 billion results in 0.51 seconds. There are charities, agencies, academic departments, legal firms, forums, blogs, Quora threads, advice columns, YouTube talks, and self-help books. Everyone has an opinion. Everyone has a story.

Adoption is big business—and also an emotional minefield.

Even the UK government has a detailed adoption section on its website, with eligibility criteria, assessment info, agency contacts, legal rights of birth parents, and support for adoptees. Since 2015, the Adoption Support Fund (ASF) has pumped nearly £200 million into therapeutic services for adoptees up to age 21. You can now apply for up to £5,000 a year for support. In contrast, in the early 1960s, there was... nothing. Had those resources existed then, who knows what difference they might have made?

Long after my adoption broke down, I would stay up late typing my birth mother's name—*So Kam Lai*—into various search engines. First Yahoo. Then AltaVista. Ask Jeeves. Netscape. Then Google. (Yes, I've been through them all.) Sometimes I'd reverse the order, entering *Lai So Kam*, placing her family name first as the Chinese do. Each time I'd hit return, there'd be this strange, fizzy blend of hope and dread. *Today might be the day I find her.* And always—nothing.

It's funny, really. You can Google "how to fix a leaking tap" and get 23 options with video tutorials. But search for your lost mother, your origin, your self? Just a blinking cursor.

Answering questions about adoption means navigating a terrain full of shifting feelings. Some emotions take years to name. Others arrive sharp and early, demanding to be heard. People want happy endings. But the truth? Adoption isn't a fairytale. It's complicated. It's often messy. And it doesn't end when the papers are signed.

Now feels like the right time to tell it straight. To show what it was *really* like. Not as a sweeping, universal statement—but from the inside of one life. Mine.

Each of the memories that follows is a puzzle piece. Not the whole picture, but part of it. A glimpse into what it meant to grow up caught between worlds—and the slow, determined journey to feel whole.

What Was It Like? Earliest Memories

Aged 15 months. I arrive in the UK. 6th February 1962.

This is how I 'remember' my beginning. A blend of hazy early memories and family anecdotes, passed down like softened facts. What's real, what was told to me, and what I might have imagined—at this point, it all blends.

My new forever family had arrived at Heathrow, enthusiastic and excited. They didn't own a car, so they travelled from Leamington Spa to London by train. It was a big day out—with me as the grand finale. An extra bonus. A real treat for my future siblings.

For my mother, my arrival marked the end of months of waiting and, perhaps, made up a little for the disappointment she had recorded in her letters to the National Children's Home. In them, she politely pleaded for news of her "replacement baby," apologising for the bother, as though she were chasing up a missing parcel.

She'd been tantalisingly close before. The first allocated baby, Gam Fong Toy, had been abruptly withdrawn at the last minute—too ill to travel. And so, the Enocks came, full of hope, ready to love.

In response to her renewed plea, my mother had been sent a tiny black-and-white passport headshot of me, taken when I first entered Po Leung Kuk Orphanage at ten weeks. Out of focus. Unsmiling. A ghost of a face. In contrast, the case file I eventually received in 2019 from the National Children's Home (now Action for Children) included two 6"x4" full-length photographs of the girl who should have come. Gam Fong Toy. She looked pretty, confident, appealing. I stared at her image for ages. Where are you now, Fong Toy?

The exhausted BOAC stewardess who'd supervised my 24-hour journey was eager to hand me over. She told my new parents I had cried almost continuously. I had wailed each time I was jolted awake from fragile sleep into the strangeness of new terminals, roaring engines, bright lights, new smells.

By the time I was finally placed into my new mother's arms, I was snivelling, shaking and screaming. My new family—white, smiling, unfamiliar—must have been bewildering. Although I had spent time with the Starkeys, my British foster family in Hong Kong, the Enocks were yet another group of strangers. Nothing about this world made sense.

The stewardess had tried to make me presentable. I was wrapped in a white acrylic furry coat and matching hat with bobbing pom-poms. A tiny snowball with red-rimmed eyes.

My new siblings watched, equal parts fascinated and repelled, as their long-awaited baby sister shoved the head of a Paddington Bear chocolate bar into her mouth. A peace offering, maybe. The crying stopped. My mouth was instantly rammed full. I had bitten off more than I could chew. Chocolate and saliva oozed out, mixing with snot and tears.

Then I wiped the whole sticky mess across my face, down the white coat, and all over the Enock children's hands and jumpers.

Living with the Enocks wasn't easy—for any of us.

On my first night, I pulled myself up using the cot bars and began rocking the metal-and-wood frame violently, banging it against the bedroom wall. Bang. Bang. Bang. This continued not just through the night, but for many nights. Weeks. My dad gave up trying to patch the crumbling plaster.

Someone—probably both my parents in shifts—would have kept getting up, trying to stop the racket. Someone had to deal with the excrement I smeared regularly on the walls. Someone had to feed me, bathe me, dress me, even though I refused to settle. According to the books, a 15-month-old should've been "sleeping through." I clearly hadn't read the manual.

It's hard now to fully grasp the fear and confusion I must have felt during those first weeks—but I suspect the sense of not quite belonging, of being always slightly out of place, took root then.

That rocking, that stink, the endless nights and the slow adjustment to my new formula—Ostermilk—and my Great British life.

I imagine it now with equal parts sorrow and a wry sort of humour. I'd arrived like a jetlagged, sticky, grief-stricken whirlwind. Not quite the bundle of joy they'd hoped for. More like a storm in a pom-pom hat.

But I was here. And the story had begun.

Getting to Grips with Adoption. What Was It Like? The Official Story

The official story goes something like this…

I have a letter my adoptive mother wrote about my progress soon after I arrived in the UK. It reports that the Enock family would not part with me for anything and that there was no bad feeling or jealousy anywhere.

Mrs. Gregory, the social worker for our family, passed on this encouraging missive to the four organisations involved in my adoption. She made many visits to the Enocks, all documented in a stack of similarly favourable reports—piles of almost transparent, now fading pale blue sheets that are as old as I am. Each line, typewritten with care, creates an illusion of everything being right and true, contrasting sharply with the faint handwritten comments, in pencil, scrawled across some of the documents. Tip tap, tip tap. I can imagine the person at the typewriter, their fingers dancing lightly over the keys. Optimistic words flying across the world and back again, keeping everyone informed of how well I was doing. Tip tap, tip tap—so bright and breezy in tone. All was well.

Everyone wanted everything to look perfect on paper—my progress, my parents' care, my siblings' adjustment. The Enocks wouldn't part with me for anything, they said. It's almost funny now, looking at those reports and comparing them to my own memories, which were far messier and far less certain. But those reports served a purpose—they made everyone feel that things were moving smoothly, that the pieces were falling into place. It was all so reassuring. Too reassuring, perhaps.

Mrs. Gregory came bearing gifts for my siblings. She was a kind, generous, and well-intentioned lady, bringing a tin toy car for my brother to ease any bad feelings he might, quite reasonably, have had, and a rag doll for my sister, who would have been perfectly justified in feeling some jealousy or frustration as she navigated her new place within our family. Mrs. Gregory continued her visits until my parents were finally allowed to adopt me in November 1963. Initially, I had been temporarily boarded out with the Enocks "with a view to adoption." When they applied to adopt me, what should have been a simple process became complicated and protracted.

My birth mother in Hong Kong had given only blanket consent for adoption by anyone deemed fit by the Director of Social Services in Hong Kong. However, English law required specific individuals—namely, the Enocks—to be named in my mother's consent.

The County Court Judge handling my case ordered that my birth mother be tracked down to provide specific consent for the Enocks to adopt me. There are numerous letters on file between Hong Kong and British social services arguing about this instruction, and the tone of those letters is far less bright and breezy. Tip tap, tip tap—the letters flew back and forth across continents, full of legal jargon and bureaucratic calm, yet beneath it all, there was an undercurrent of fear. The reality of tracking down my birth mother, someone who might want me back, wasn't something anyone wanted to confront.

It was easier to keep things neat, to type away as if this was all just part of the process. But of course, life—real life—never fits so tidily into forms and reports.

Eventually, Hong Kong social services reported that they had tried and failed to locate my mother at her last known address. To circumvent the issue, I was made a ward of court, and my guardian ad litem consented to my adoption. Tick, tick, tick—job done. Everyone was happy.

Kind Mrs. Gregory also wrote on my mother's behalf to the National Children's Home (NCH), one of the organisations involved in my adoption. She described how my parents were struggling financially and could not afford to buy me a bed. In response, the NCH sent my mother a cheque for £10. We were not a well-off family, but no doubt I was, as I was so often told, better off with the Enocks than if I'd remained in an orphanage.

I thrived on my Ostermilk and welfare orange juice, grew into my sister's hand-me-downs, and twirled in the dresses my mother sewed from remnants. I excelled at school, Brownies, and ballet. I was the only child in my school to pass the 11-plus—not just any pass, but a full scholarship to a prestigious school. I was a child who won medals for dancing and had my photo featured in the local paper. I learned to play the piano and performed on stage, relishing being the centre of attention. Which was just as well, as I was frequently in the spotlight—just a small

Chinese girl bobbing about, putting on a big smile for a sea of curious white British faces.

Getting to Grips with Adoption. What Was It like? Happy School Days

In the primary school playground, and up my street, I had the chance to make new friends—but being adopted, being the only Chinese kid in a sea of white British faces, wasn't exactly easy. Chinese, in NHS specs, second-hand clothes, and a donated bed—yet top of the class. If they'd been measuring ethnic minority achievement back then, I'd have skewed the stats single-handedly.

Child A : "What's your name?"

Me : "LawlaEnock."

Child A : "What's your name?"

Me : "Lawla, LawlaEnock."

Child A : "WHAT?"

Me : Lawla. "My name's LawlaEnock."

Child A : Where do you come from?

Me : *Silence*

Child A : "Is your dad a Chink then?"

Child A : "Where's your mum from?"

Me : *Silence*

Child A : "Chinese, Japanese, Dirty Knees, what are these?" (Loudly, singing, laughing and pulling at his eyes) "Chinese, Japanese, Dirty Knees, what are these?"

Me : "What's your name?"

Child A : "Four eyed chink, four eyed chink. Hey, come and look at four eyed chink!" "Chinese, Japanese, Dirty Knees, what are these?"

Child B : "Enoch, Enoch, Enoch Powell. Your dad's Enoch Powell."

At eight years old, I had no real idea who Enoch Powell was—or why strangers questioned me about my surname. Didn't I mean Enoch with an "h," not Enock with a "k"? How does a little Chinese girl tell a big English adult that yes, she really does know how to spell her surname—but the Chinese name she's only ever seen written down once feels far more uncertain?

The name "Enoch Powell" meant nothing to me. I didn't really care. I was too busy trying to understand why children threw stones at me when I rode my bike. The chant of "four-eyed Chink, go home" hurt more than the stones ever did.

As I grew older, I got better at spotting who might become a friend and who was best avoided. I reasoned that Mr Relf, the man who lived down our street and plastered placards in his garden reading "Whites United Against Coloured Invasion" and "For Sale Only to an English Family," was probably someone to steer clear of. He might not throw stones, but I doubted he'd welcome my presence.

When the TV crew came to our street to film Mr Relf for Midlands Today, other children ran out to gawk. I stayed indoors. Silent. Hidden.

What Was It Like Being Adopted? Out of the Woods. A Therapeutic Story

I first wrote *Baby Bear Has a Bad Day* many years ago, while training to be a counsellor. At the time, I didn't think of it as a therapeutic story. I only knew that a memory inside me felt too heavy to carry, too painful to face head-on. So I gave it to a small bear. Putting my feelings into her paws allowed me to hold them at a distance, close enough to honour but far enough to bear.

Later in life, I discovered therapeutic story writing, a model created by Dr Trisha Waters, and realised what I had done without knowing: I had written my own therapeutic story. In my work with children, I watched how they too could use story to shape feelings too big to name. Through imagination and metaphor, they found not only healing but also the joy of discovering themselves as writers. I will never forget the way their faces lit up when they realised their words mattered. Confidence in writing is its own kind of magic, and as a writer myself, I know how precious that gift can be.

Like the children, I still find that stories make hard truths softer to touch. Each time I revisit Baby Bear, the sadness that once reduced me to tears grows lighter. What once felt unbearable has become a companion I can sit beside, gently, on the page.

Baby Bear Has a Bad Day

Once upon a time, there was a bear family who lived in a small town in middle England. Daddy Bear was a stores man, and Mummy Bear was training to be a teacher. They had three small bear cubs. This story takes place one autumn in the woods, when the eldest boy cub was about 10, the middle girl cub was 8, and the littlest baby girl cub was 6. The family didn't have a lot of money, so a walk in the woods to go blackberry picking was a treat they could afford. Everyone had sturdy boots and warm woollen coats. Baby Bear was bundled in her big brother's old coat, the sleeves too long, swallowing her small hands, and the boots too large and heavy, making her stumble as they all trudged over the crackling leaves. Baby Bear enjoyed the unfamiliar scent of damp soil and fallen foliage.

The bear cubs were excited, their chatter mingling with the rustle of leaves. The two eldest had already talked about what Mummy Bear and Daddy Bear might make with the berries. Baby Bear heard the words "apple and blackberry pie" and saw her big sister's eyes shine with excitement. She had no idea what pie was—she was from a different country called China and had been brought up on rice porridge and noodles. And when Baby Bear looked in the mirror, she could tell she wasn't quite the same as her brother and sister, but nobody ever talked much about where she had come from or why.

Mummy Bear and Daddy Bear told her she would not be going anywhere anytime soon—that she would stay with her new family forever and ever. Sometimes Baby Bear puzzled over why they had chosen her, especially when they seemed so worried about money. She knew it had taken a lot of sorting out for them to get the money for her to come and live in their house. And every now and then, a Social Worker Bear would visit to check that all the cubs were happy. The cubs knew to play nicely when Social Worker Bear came. Before leaving, Social Worker Bear would speak with Mummy Bear in the hall, and a few days later, a letter would arrive saying they could keep Baby Bear.

Once they were in the woods, Mummy Bear gave each cub a pot to collect berries and warned them not to eat any—especially the pink ones, which weren't ripe. Baby Bear didn't know what ripe meant, but she was too excited to ask. She wandered off, happily picking berries. And, of course, she couldn't resist trying a few. She was proud to fill her cup with shiny blackberries and went running back to Mummy Bear to show her.

But Mummy Bear was not pleased. She saw the stains on Baby Bear's mouth. "Why does she never do what she's told?" she snapped at Daddy Bear. "I expect you've eaten some pink ones as well, haven't you?" she shouted at Baby Bear.

Baby Bear was confused. She couldn't remember if she had but thought Mummy Bear would be pleased if she agreed. So she cried and said, "Yes, I did."

"Well," said Mummy Bear, her voice sharp and cutting, "then you're going to die. The pink ones are poisonous. I told you not to eat them, and now look what you've done. You're going to die."

The other two cubs began to dance around her, chanting, "You're going to die, die, you're going to die!"

Baby Bear didn't know what pie was, but she knew what "die" and "poisonous" meant. The family's pet cat had died only the week before.

Mummy Bear had said someone had poisoned it when they'd found it in the garden, all manky and stiff with blood coming out of its nose.

"I don't want to die," sobbed Baby Bear. "Please take me to hospital."

But none of the bear family comforted her. The two cubs kept dancing, and even Daddy Bear—who was usually kind to Baby Bear, especially when Mummy Bear wasn't around—just stood by, silent.

Baby Bear sobbed harder. She screamed so much that snot and dribble covered her face and hands, smeared with purple juice from the berries. That made her even more scared.

"Please take me to hospital," she screamed again. She knew hospital was where you went to be mended. Mummy Bear and Daddy Bear had taken her there once before, to get her eye stitched up after a tickling game went wrong and she'd hit her face on the corner of the heater.

She collapsed onto the forest floor and curled up in a ball, sobbing. Why wouldn't someone save her?

Then she felt big hands around her shaking body. Someone picked her up. It was Daddy Bear. She heard him say, "It's alright, they're only joking. You're not going to die."

Baby Bear smiled. She smiled through her tears. She smiled because she'd learned that smiling was what you did to make everyone feel better.

But after that—once she got out of the woods—she never quite trusted that bear family, or anyone else, ever again.

Getting to Grips with Adoption. Rejection

Well-meaning friends, keen to know more about what had caused my estrangement from my adoptive family, would ask, "What did you do?" instead of "What happened?" The latter suggested a shared responsibility for the breakup, while the former implied it was something I had engineered all by myself. Even my children, when they were young, asked questions like, "What did you do to your family, Mummy, that we never see our granny or our aunt who live around the corner?" My husband, Martin once told me he suspected I had done something terrible that was too awful to admit.

Memoir writing, especially this part, is tough. I knew it would be, but how can it be this hard? Five days into this chapter so far, and I have nothing to show except a screwed-up face from scrutinising things I'd much rather forget. How do I make sense of something I've never understood, let alone shape it into something coherent that readers can grasp and, like me, struggle to emotionally fathom?

I'm not writing in a vacuum. Here I sit, a privileged writer in my pale lemon office, at a custom-built desk that goes up and down—yes, it does. Comfortable in Martin's "Magic Life" office chair, a throne with more levers than a cockpit, built to make your spine feel like royalty. I find my MacBook Air perched on a matching silver metal stand. This perfect ergonomic setup is meant to make writing pain-free and a breeze. Ha! My head throbs, likely brought on by all that discursive thinking about life back then—life in the 1970s, living in a decrepit double-fronted townhouse my parents bought when I was sixteen. Rooms with gaping holes where ceilings and floors should be. Window frames bare of any paint, some so rotten the glass would fall out if you tried to open them. Foul cracked toilets and stained basins with no taps. Corroded handrails everywhere. Anything of value, like copper pipes, lead off the roof, and electrical fittings had been ripped out and sold for scrap. There was no kitchen, and the huge garden lay hidden under thick brambles and weeds, abandoned white goods, broken bicycles, and old mattresses. It was once a glorious Regency townhouse but had been carved up by a council required to provide emergency homes for desperate people. This was to be our family home. I remember thinking it was, like me, another rescue project for my mum.

I start by trying to write about the time my mum crossed the road to avoid speaking to me. By then, I was married and had already endured five years of rejection. I had persuaded my husband to buy our first marital home just around the corner from my old childhood house. What on earth was I thinking?

As I ponder why she crossed the road to avoid me—and why I bought a house around the corner from the family who wouldn't speak to me—my daughter Lucy video calls me from a road trip to an Italian wedding, seeking reassurance. Someone who, as she puts it, runs with her tribe. We talk briefly, and I feel elated as I hear the rising confidence in her voice and the lively banter between us. But moments later, I deflate and become tearful. My then and now collide as I realise that for years, I have excused my mother's bizarre behaviour by telling myself, "A girl doesn't need her mother after she's 18." Yet Lucy still wants and needs me, her mother. Occasionally, she needs practical help, but more often, she contacts me to share her good news or for encouragement and emotional support. Lucy is nearly 30.

And I wanted my mother. Despite my attempts to convince myself otherwise, even as a married woman, I craved something—anything—that resembled a mother-daughter relationship with that woman.

Through my tears, the voice shifts. Third person now. *The girl.*

One of their last encounters.

That woman. My adoptive mother. Me. Mid twenties.

That woman across the road. Dr Scholl sandals. White socks hanging around her ankles. Drab slacks. Shapeless cardigan. A cigarette between her fingers. Grey straggly hair. Black plastic shoulder bag.

She could be anyone. But the girl knows. This is her mother. Correction: was her mother.

The girl feels five. But she is married now. Has a house of her own. She steps off the kerb, towards her. A voice in her head: *This will set you back. Weeks to recover.*

Friends say: make up with your mother. You'll regret it otherwise. As if she hasn't tried. Telephone calls cut short. Letters unanswered. A door slammed in her face.

It is like standing in front of a juggernaut. And being crushed.

Still she crosses. Popping out for milk. Now inches away from her mother.

"Sorry, Mum."

The words hang in the air.

Which mum? Whose mum? Who should be apologising to whom? Her mother was adopted too. Her own mother had abandoned her. Perhaps more than one apology is needed. From all the mothers who were missing. Who left. Who failed.

The girl takes another step. Not to touch her. There has never been touching. No photographs either. She just wants to be closer. Like a moth to a flame.

Her mother draws on the cigarette. Looks through her, not at her. Eyes hard behind smeared lenses. A face that turns away.

Her gift: her back.

The girl does not think, *I can't wait to see the back of you.* Her hand pulls back of its own accord. She knows it would only make things worse if she tried to stop her.

The kerb is awkward. But her mother manages it. Steps down into the gutter. Passes her own child. Crosses away.

Author's Note: The only way I could get to the end of this was to write in the third person. I erased myself from the piece, just as my mother had erased me from her life. Perhaps we both manage our pain by erasure? I continue that day writing in the third person. It is as if I'm writing about a stranger. That way, I have a chance of reaching the end of this part of my memoir.

A Forgotten Birthday. Aged Five or Six.

Her family had forgotten her birthday, and throughout the day, the little girl tried to convince herself they were planning a surprise for teatime. But as the hours passed, her hopes faded. Teatime came and went.

That night, in bed, she resorted to her old habit of sucking her thumb—to soothe herself, to muffle the sobs.

She'd brought that bad habit with her all the way from Hong Kong. In the early years, her right thumb was often sore and bleeding. Her family told her time and again to stop, warning that if she didn't, her big teeth would come through all crooked.

On the night of the forgotten birthday, she started sucking again.

Eventually, she was fitted with a hard plastic plate and wire clips on her teeth. Her mother, of course, had plenty of "I told you so's" to offer.

A Family Outing. Age Six or Seven?

In my recollection, I appear as a young child of around 6 or 7, even though I was likely older.

The images in my mind paint a vivid picture of that day. Together, like characters from a scene in *Mary Poppins*, the children lined up at the Midland Bank. Each clutching their cherished gold-embossed savings passbook, they eagerly reached up to the high wooden counter, sliding it through the narrow slot in the thick plate glass. The youngest child, determined and proud, stood on tiptoe to complete the task. The kind bank lady marked "closed" on several pages, returning the passbook along with a small stack of notes and coins. The children's savings were contributing to the deposit for the big house their parents were striving to purchase. With each deposit, they inched closer to their mother's cherished dream of owning a family home where, in the future, they would all reside as adults with their own families. Their mother reassured them, "It's the next best thing to my dream of running a children's home."

I believed in the dream mum sold us—that our savings were building something secure and lasting. But when I stepped into that house, years later, it was crumbling, hollowed out. A rescue project, like me. Full of hope on paper. But the reality didn't match the promise.

Feigning Sickness. Aged Seven.

She was young—and whether it was due to indulging in too many sweets (unlikely, as her family didn't have much to spend on confectionery) or a stomach bug—the girl found herself hunched over a bowl. Her dad was by her side, scraping back her hair.

There was less hair for him to hold now. Her mum had recently given it a furious trim after the girl whined, "That hurts, mummy" one too many times while being brushed. Out of patience, her mum had yanked her hair into a ponytail with a rubber band and chopped it clean off. The long, lustrous ponytail—once adorned with a shiny orange bow—reduced to a blunt, sad stump.

That same bow had gone with her to Ted Mayman's barber shop, a bustling little place at the edge of town, full of men in old leather side chairs reading newspapers. On a rare solo outing with her dad, Ted had perched her high on a leather stool and spun her theatrically for the audience. Draped in a vast black cape, she emerged from its folds like a small Chinese warrior. The customers glanced up from their newspapers and smiled, delighted. Arthur Enock's little girl—who'd have thought it?

A bright, showstopping, orange-beribboned centrepiece in the middle of a man's world.

But today, there was no theatre. The girl had vomited all over the candlewick bedspread. Her mother stood in the doorway, arms crossed, lips pursed. She said something sharp—something to her dad about her pretending to be ill and doing it to deliberately to make them argue, something that the girl didn't fully understand but felt, like a slap without contact.

The girl is seven.

Perhaps this was the beginning. The first time she was cast not just as difficult, but as the reason. Why they fought, why things didn't feel right. A small child absorbing what no child should: that love can twist, that blame can land where it does not belong.

In the barber's shop she was the centre of delight —shiny bow, small warrior, admired and adored. Behind closed doors, the shine faded. Something darker crept in. Not fear. Not anger. Only the quiet, creeping belief that she was wrong. That the trouble in the room was her fault.

Overdose and Expulsion. Aged Seventeen.

She hadn't planned to fail. She had been the model pupil, the scholarship girl with Cambridge in sight. But the cracks began to show in small, unnoticed ways. The new house her parents had bought during her O levels swallowed their attention. The school pushed her into a Greek A level class a year too advanced, where she floundered like a fish out of water, already doomed to fail. At home her mother said university was pointless, a waste of time. At school the message was different: reach higher, aim for Cambridge. Between them she was stranded, unheard. And then she fell in love for the first time—with a boy who wasn't one of the nice boys from the boys' version of their posh school, but one who took drugs.

The writing was on the wall, but nobody was reading.

Fast forward ten years from the feigning sickness episode and the now teenage girl is undeniably very sick. She is in hospital from an accidental recreational amphetamine overdose. For months she has been experimenting with drugs—cannabis, LSD and speed—and truanting from school. Her descent from being an excellent, high-achieving student has been swift, yet unnoticed by her family or teachers. She can forge her mother's signature on an absence note with ease; she's done it so many times. She fails all her mock exams. It's only a matter of time before events reach a breaking point.

Somebody finds her late one night, unconscious and convulsing, blood streaming from a hole in her tongue that she has bitten right through during an intense seizure. The family doctor comes; there are more convulsions. He calls an ambulance, and she is rushed to hospital.

A week or so later, once again on her own, she faces her headteacher and deputy head who, with polite regret, inform her that she is expelled from the posh girls' school where she was studying Greek, Latin and English. The school that had once encouraged her to apply for Cambridge to read Classics. Strangely, the news comes as a relief.

Luckily, the girl regains consciousness and recovers completely. Both of her parents are at work when she comes to, but her sister is there and her mum has left her a letter written meticulously in that familiar copperplate handwriting the girl had spent countless hours perfecting through forgery. The letter describes in vivid detail what had happened—a late-night doctor's call-out, an ambulance with blue flashing lights and siren racing her to hospital. Her mother cautions her not to lie to protect those who had given her the drugs. The letter concludes with "We all love you, my darling." The girl is comforted to have that in writing, those words her mum has never ever said aloud. She rereads that line repeatedly, secretly wishing her mum had used "I" instead of "we", as that would have meant something more.

A nurse comes to check her temperature and the hole in her tongue and to run a few tests. She tells her patient that she's lucky to be alive. Apparently, she gave them all such a fright and the admissions team had been concerned she might die or be permanently brain-damaged.

The girl never knew exactly how the school found out about her overdose. Later, someone said a fellow pupil's father had been the hospital registrar on duty when she was admitted—an unfortunate twist of fate. What troubled her most wasn't that she might have died, or that she couldn't transfer to another school to continue her A-levels, or even who had told the school. What lingered was this: that her best friend, who had also taken drugs, had also been expelled. But her friend had not had to attend any disciplinary meeting. Her parents went in her place. But the girl—just seventeen, still recovering from a near-fatal overdose—was made to go alone. She sat across from two adult women, her headteacher and deputy head, and was politely asked to leave.

And then, just days later, came the knock at the door.

Her best friend's parents stood on the grey stone doorstep, wild-eyed and furious. The two adults she had once secretly wished could have been her own parents. They had taken her on as one of the family, invited her to dinner, taken her to the theatre, welcomed her into their grand home with its enormous garden and ride-on mower. Her friend's mother wore a wide-brimmed hat, secured with a chiffon scarf, and tended roses in kid leather gloves. Her father gave his daughter the latest tech—a yellow cassette player with shared headphones. On warm summer afternoons, the girls would sit on the white wooden swing seat, earphones pressed together, revising for O-levels while listening to The Carpenters.

Now those same parents stand on her doorstep.

The girl was still weak, alone in the house again. She opened the door, and they came at her like a storm. The mother, usually so composed, was sobbing, streaked mascara and blotchy skin beneath her

Lancôme foundation. The father, usually mild-mannered, bared his teeth and shouted in her face, gesturing wildly with clenched fists. In that moment, the girl genuinely thought he might hit her.

They had come straight from the school meeting and wanted her to know their daughter had also been expelled—and that it was *her* fault. That she had ruined their daughter's life. That weight—of blame, of rage, of grief—was dumped squarely on the shoulders of a teenage girl who had nearly died the week before.

Now THAT was a big responsibility to dump on a recovering seventeen-year-old.

Flowers for Mother.

The girl had to find a job. Nobody told her she had to. But she couldn't sit around the house, afraid of ruining any more lives now that she was on the road to recovery. She landed a job easily. The employment agency told her it was right up her street—an administrative position at the BSJA (British Show Jumping Association) that paid £1500 per annum. Money enough to pay her mum some rent and have some left over for clothes and makeup.

Thirty-five hours of her week were now spent colouring pictures of horses and adding stars on their foreheads or white socks to their hooves—maddening, but oddly therapeutic. She found a sense of ease being surrounded by these women who lived and breathed horses and loved their jobs, even though she loved neither. They were friendly and kind to her, but it was another place where she didn't quite fit.

One of her colleagues, Ann, was saving up to buy a new horse trailer. She supplemented her wages by making hanging baskets and plant tub arrangements that she brought into the office to sell. On special days the office became a vibrant nursery, bustling with workers from neighbouring units eager to add a touch of green to their lives. It added welcome variety to the non-stop horse talk.

Mother's Day was Ann's busiest time, and she persuaded the girl that a floral arrangement would make a thoughtful gift. With great care, the girl chose one: blue hyacinths and bright yellow daffodils, all neatly planted in a long green trough. She cradled it in her lap on the bus ride home, the smell of earth and flowers curling up around her like hope.

But when she presented it to her mother, the reaction was far from what she'd imagined. Her mother accused her of deliberately trying to harm her. "You know I'm allergic to hyacinths!" she shouted. The girl did not. "What are you trying to do—kill me?" The trough was hurled into the cellar with the rubbish.

The girl's heart sank. What would it take to win her mother's approval, to bridge the divide between them?

And yet—even after everything—she'd tried. She had picked something lovely. She had carried it home with care. That mattered.

The next day, Ann asked, "Did your mum like her present?"

"Oh, yes," the girl lied, putting on her bravest face. "I'm sure she loved it."

Threads of rejection ran through everything.

And yet between the silences and the shouting, something fragile began to grow.

Recovery

Getting Some Help. Early twenties.

The Relate offices in Leamington Spa were in such a sorry state they were under threat of demolition. Gloomy, high-ceilinged rooms. Grimy windows. Wingback chairs that had seen better decades. Beige woodchip wallpaper peeled from damp walls like skin from a blister. And yet, it was here that the young woman first began to get help.

She met weekly with Hilary, and later with Maureen when Hilary retired. Hilary was the first of many counsellors she would encounter in her life. An hour a week, on and off, for three years. Crying her way through strategically placed tissue boxes, trying to make sense of herself. Of the self-destructive relationships. The aching need to be loved. The confusion. The rage. And the relentless shame of not being the girl she was supposed to be.

Back then, she didn't yet connect the rejection by her family with her clutch of failed relationships. She hadn't yet made the link between being taken in as an orphan—promised love forever—and then discarded, as if faulty. Or maybe she had. But it felt too big, too bleak, too treacherous to say aloud.

So instead she talked about the boyfriends. The heartbreak. The longing. She talked in circles, because that's what trauma does—it loops and repeats until the shape starts to make sense.

Everyone had always told her how grateful she should be. Grateful to have been adopted "by such a nice family." The message was spelt out slowly, carefully, as if she were dim. It had been drummed into her, again and again: she'd been lucky. Chosen. Saved. But she didn't feel grateful. And that, in itself, became something else to feel ashamed about.

So hard to be grateful in a room emptied of love.

One day, perhaps defying all professional norms, her counsellor Maureen leaned forward, likely breaking the rules "You know," she said almost conspiratorially, "I don't think I like your mother."

The young woman cried for the rest of the hour. A box of tissues gone, her sleeve soaked through.

Getting Some More Help. Aged 36.

Around fifteen years later, the young woman (although she is no longer young, being 36 years old and married with two small children) finds herself in another counselling session. This time, the setting is quite different from Relate. It is a modern, well-lit space with low, cushioned chairs, side tables, and large windows adorned with vertical blinds. Abstract prints hang on the walls, and a white Ikea coffee table holds tissues, water, artificial flowers, and informational brochures about the services offered at the holistic centre.

But the change in surroundings does nothing to soften the inner chaos. This is her third session with her counsellor May. She is desperate. She has just left her marital home—walked out on her husband, her children, the life she built. After having an affair.

Until a month ago, she was seen as the ideal mother, a church volunteer, a Girl Guide leader, holding everything together. Sometimes she almost believed it herself, though the role never felt like it belonged to her, had she done enough to deserve it? Now, she's living alone in a rented room, hollowed-out by guilt, confused by her own actions, and paralysed by shame. How could she have done this? What kind of mother leaves?

The counsellor, May, is calm and nurturing. She does not flinch at the torrent of tears. She doesn't offer false comfort either. Instead, she gently speaks of something called attachment theory.

As the woman sobs, May introduces the idea of *attachment*. That sometimes the relationships we form as adults are shaped by the relationships we had as children. She explains how, when early attachments are unpredictable or absent or wounding, they can make it difficult to feel safe or secure later on. That seeking love outside a marriage might not be about lust or recklessness—it might be about hunger. For connection. For reassurance. For a sense of being seen.

"It's the way our earliest relationships shape how we connect with others," May explains, her voice low and kind. "If a baby isn't met with consistent love and soothing, she adapts. She might learn to keep her needs hidden. Or to chase love desperately, afraid it will disappear. Or both."

The woman nods, tears slipping steadily down her cheeks. May continues, "When love is unpredictable, or frightening, it teaches us to mistrust closeness—even while we long for it. That's what we call disorganised attachment. It's not your fault. It's a survival strategy. It's what helped you get through."

The woman lets out a shaky breath. It is the first time someone has connected the dots so clearly. Her affair, her paralysis, her panic—these things begin to shift from shameful evidence of her brokenness into something else: messages. Clues. Coping mechanisms.

May stays right there alongside the woman, down in the detritus of it all. And so the woman stays. She cries. She listens. And something begins, ever so faintly, to change.

A Bit of a Showdown. Aged 20.

In the counselling sessions, this memory surfaced again and again—the final encounter with my family.

I was on the doorstep of our home, going home to visit. Dread and determination twisting in me. The etched glass panels on the heavy green door had cracked more since my last visit. With a shaking hand, I pressed the bell.

They were waiting. My mother, five feet of fury, flanked by my towering siblings. My father behind them, shifting uneasily, caught in a fight he didn't want. Together they formed a barricade. Their silence pressed in, thick and airless. I wanted to scream but swallowed it down.

At last, my father spoke: "Why haven't you come to see us before?"

I looked down at the dirty floor and surprised us all. "It hasn't been that long. Why haven't any of you come to see me?"

Until then, I had never answered back. Usually I froze, or fled in tears, only to be punished afterwards. My mother's way was to send me to Coventry: first the lash of words that cut me down, then silence. Days, sometimes weeks of it. Later, the silence gave way to slaps—sharp, private blows—and now she was training the others to follow her lead.

That day, I turned and left. The door slammed behind me, sealing our estrangement for the next thirty-four years.

A Lightbulb Moment. Aged 55.

Little did I know, standing on that doorstep, that it would take three and a half decades of silence before a light finally flickered on, showing me it wasn't my fault.

It is 2015. My parents have both been dead for a year. Both gone within months of each other, after decades of living under the same roof without speaking.

I organise my father's funeral. My brother and sister help too and attend but it's all made harder because they are estranged. Unable to be reunited even as he lay dying, or to mourn him together. My sister arranges my mother's funeral—and this time, neither my brother nor I are invited. I attend anyway. There is no mention of us during the service, nor in the thick albums of photos and stories my sister has prepared to celebrate my mum's life. It is as if we never existed.

My brother and I are disinherited. My father never signed his final will—the one that would have divided everything of his between the three of us. Instead, an old will is upheld, leaving it all to my mother, who then leaves it all to my sister. I don't know how to grieve any of it. Numbness gives way to anger, sadness, disbelief. Round and round in circles.

One day, I spread a paper tablecloth across the kitchen table and begin to draw a genogram, as I once did for my therapy clients. Not just a family tree, but a map of connections—and disconnections.

And suddenly, I see it.

This family had been tearing itself apart for years. My parents, estranged under the same roof. My brother estranged from my mother. My sister estranged from my father. My siblings estranged from each other.

It was never just me.

For decades I had carried a question that was never mine to answer.

No.

It wasn't about what I had done or failed to do. I was a casualty of something broken long before me.

I breathe out, as if for the first time.

The Enocks gave me the basics—home, education, support of sorts. But not love. The unconditional kind. Perhaps they had never known how.

Not all of this was about me. Not all of it was my fault.

How could I have ever believed I was so powerful as to bring down an entire family?

And if I didn't belong with the Enocks... then with whom did I belong?

One Last Shot.

When it finally dawns on you that you have every reason to keep searching for your birth family, and even the slimmest chance remains, who do you turn to?

I had rarely considered how my children might feel about having no connection to their Chinese heritage. Perhaps I did, briefly, when they came home with family-tree drawings that showed glaring holes where their maternal grandparents should have been. Despite reconnecting with my adoptive dad, Arthur, they had only met him a few times.

As a young mother, I kept myself busy, holding back my most difficult feelings. My first husband, Andrew, tried to bridge the gap—he even attempted to talk to my mother, but she refused. Andrew and I worked together to keep our small family safe, but deep down I lived with a longing and an ache I couldn't name. One Christmas morning, my confused five-year-old son said, *"Mummy's crying again, Daddy."* His words echo still.

Fast forward twenty-five years. After therapy, training, and painful lessons, I was older, wiser, and finally beginning to understand how my early experiences had shaped me. Studying Bowlby's attachment theory brought me back to those counselling sessions with May. I was learning to be kinder to myself.

With new clarity, some income, and time on my hands, I decided to search again. Not just for my birth family, but for the version of myself who might have existed under different circumstances. I wanted my children to feel more rooted, to have a clearer sense of identity and belonging.

A friend suggested I apply to the TV show *Long Lost Family*. I'd never heard of it, but their website said they specialised in difficult cases where the trail had gone cold. Their team could access official records and international archives unavailable to the general public. It sounded promising.

My first application was rejected. Two years later, my daughter Lucy sent me a short, heartfelt text after hearing I'd organised a reunion in St Ives for Hong Kong adoptees. Just three sentences—but enough to spur me on. I applied again, more carefully. This time, they said yes.

I signed legal documents and agreed to stop searching myself. For over a year, emails trickled in from the production team: they were working on my case. But in time I learned they had made little progress. Winnie Siu Davies, a key Hong Kong adoptee advocate they had contacted and asked to help, insisted I be involved in any search. The show wanted a surprise reveal. Stalemate.

Then in August 2018, the search was closed by email. No phone call. No resolution. Just a kind message expressing regret, with the name of another organisation I could try.

It was a quiet heartbreak. But it didn't end my search. I told my children I would go on. That I had to.

My mother's presence lived on—in me, in them, in my granddaughter Phoebe. I would keep searching, for her and for us all.

What Are You Doing? Age 58.

It is late August 2018. The day begins bright and warm, but I am subdued. Two weeks since *Long Lost Family* gave up on me. Even the experts had run out of road.

I sit in our lofty penthouse in St Ives, gazing out at the harbour. Visitors look up and say I am living their dream. Little do they know I long for what they carry so lightly: that easy optimism, the ability to feel grateful for what is, rather than yearning for what was lost.

Their wonder is genuine. First-time visitors, seduced by Cornish dramas and documentaries, arrive unsure if the place will live up to the hype. It does. The coastline is as spectacular as Poldark's galloping cliff scenes suggest. The fishing villages do smell faintly of salt and seaweed, and yes, you really can barbecue freshly caught fish on the beach while the sun sets in streaks of crimson and gold. They raise their glasses—Polgoon fizz, crisp Sauvignon Blanc—against a mackerel sky and toast Cornish life and their good fortune.

The life I am ready and willing to leave.

The bifold doors are open, sunshine spilling in, and below I can hear the low hum of happy people drifting across the Wharf. The tide is fully out. If I took two minutes to walk to the beach, I'd find joy rippling across the sand—barefoot children running wild, families wading in turquoise water. On days like this, St Ives is luminous.

But I don't move. I sit quietly, laptop on my knees, and click.

"What are you doing?" Martin asks, as if I might be ordering lightbulbs.

"I've just booked a flight to Hong Kong."

He pauses. But to his credit, he doesn't call me mad, or sigh, or accuse me of chasing ghosts. He simply nods.

Click. Click. Card details. Three-digit code. Done. A return flight for £350, carry-on only. I will leave on November 14th. I will come back on Valentine's Day. Ninety days to search. One last shot.

A gift. From me, Laura Tan, to myself—Yuk Lan.

Accommodation? I have no budget for Hong Kong's luxury or even its modest hotels. The shabbiest Airbnb in the grimmest part of town is beyond me. But I've never needed five stars. I like street food, shared spaces, the buzz of travel. A dorm bed is fine, if it gets me where I need to be.

I text Winnie, the Hong Kong adoptee advocate introduced to me by *Long Lost Family*. She suggests a safe, no-frills area: Mody Road in Tsim Sha Tsui, Kowloon. I find a female dorm in Hop Inn Mody—eight bunks, clean and cheerful. Affordable. I book it.

Flight. Accommodation. Search partner.

Done.

For the first time, I have time—and just enough money—to return to Hong Kong and search. Not just for my family, but for the rest of myself.

If I follow this thread—delicate, almost invisible—perhaps it will lead me back to what I lost long ago. A connection that loops back to my birth mother, So Kam Lai, and forward to my daughter Lucy. And to Phoebe, who carries the soft imprint of all our stories.

And then I remember an astonishing fact: when So Kam Lai was pregnant with me, she was already carrying a part of the future. Inside me, even then, were the eggs that would become my own children.

So Kam Lai. Laura. Lucy/Tom. Three lives nested together. Three generations carried as one, if only for a while.

I close the laptop. I breathe. And I wait.

PART TWO:
90 DAYS TO FIND A LONG LOST FAMILY - BACK HOME TO HONG KONG

"Do you think I know what I'm doing? That for one breath or half-breath I belong to myself? As much as a pen knows what it's writing, or the ball can guess where it's going next."

Rumi

"You just stay here in this one corner of the Forest waiting for others to come to you. Why don't you go to them sometimes?"

AA Milne, The House at Pooh Corner

"You can leave Hong Kong, but it will never leave you."

Nury Vittachi, Hong Kong : The City of Dreams

90 Days to Search - A Blog's Backstory

When I left for Hong Kong, I hadn't planned to write a blog. I didn't know how the trip would unfold. But I did know I wanted to: a) let family and friends know I was safe and how I was getting on, b) have a consistent place to record my thoughts and feelings, and c) build a habit of daily journalling, with entries neatly date-stamped. A blog seemed to meet all those requirements.

It turned out to be my first real attempt at daily writing for an audience. Friends and family tuned in each day to check where I was, how I was doing. Afterwards, many told me how captivated they'd been—how they couldn't wait for the next update. That encouragement mattered more than they knew.

To preserve some of that immediacy, I've kept much of the blog in its raw form. Partly because I still don't quite know how to knock it into better shape, and partly because it's a testament to what can be done with an iPhone SE, a tiny folding Bluetooth keyboard, and the discipline of showing up on the page every single day.

Still, I didn't make it easy for myself. I wrote on multiple devices, across different platforms, and sometimes on whatever paper was at hand—napkins, receipts, half-filled Muji notebooks. Those scribbled, often illegible notes helped capture the spontaneity and rawness of the journey. I'm glad I tried to keep everything in one place and I'm finally learning to love 'Messy and free spirited Laura', too.

Because She's Worth It

November 14 2018.
Birmingham Airport

It seemed absolutely right that my little granddaughter of four months, Phoebe Olive Gibbs, came to give her nai nai (mandarin for paternal grandmother) the best send-off. She was waving me off to search for my roots—and hers, and Tom's, and Lucy's too. Thank you, my lovely daughter-in-law, Lisa. As I waved goodbye to Phoebe, I thought of the quiet, unspoken farewells of my own childhood—so different. Yet here I was, continuing the search for the roots we all share, even across generations.

Back to My Roots

Note to reader: please bear with me. You're now well into Part Two, but this was actually written before Part One—in real time, as a blog while I searched for my family. Occasionally the two parts overlap, but as my search progressed, so too did my understanding. As you read on, I promise things will become clearer for you, as they did for me.

November 14 2018
Birmingham Airport 17.30

Back in 1962 I arrived from Hong Kong. Alone. Today, 56 years later, I am flying back. Alone.

Where to begin a blog? How come I'm here at Birmingham airport with very little, about to fly to Hong Kong, and leave behind all that I love—my little not 'long lost family,' my dearest friends, little cat Dorey, the sea and sky of St Ives, and the green and late roses of Clopton (my family home where Tom, Lisa and Phoebe now live).

The story began so long ago, before I contacted Long Lost Family, before the idea that somebody competent was searching for my roots, before the flight I booked one Sunday afternoon, before, before...

The story began in 1959, I guess. When my widowed mother, So Kam Lai, was leaving post-Communist Mao China, along with thousands of others, including her three children—a son and two daughters. She was a refugee, heading to the shack slum hillside camps of Hong Kong. I don't know how or where she met my father, who was also fleeing mainland China. He had a wife and children too. They weren't with him. Not his wife, or those other half-siblings. I don't know how many of them there were and whether they were boys or girls. They followed on later. But by this time, I had been conceived and was just about to be born when Wong Tin—that's my father—his little family arrived. What transpired, only they must know. But my mother and father separated, and my mother took up—whatever that means—with another man, Tang Kam Wah, and I was born in a hut in Hang Shui. October 20, 1960.

I have always had a strong sense my mother loved me, had wanted to keep me, must have breastfed me, and always convinced myself she must have been heartbroken when, on December 31, 1960, she put me into *Po Leung Kuk orphanage at ten weeks old. At this point, I like to think she still believed she would get me out again. But when she was hospitalised with kidney problems, Hong Kong Social Services recommended—forced? requested? who knows?—that she should put me up for adoption. She couldn't, apparently, manage to look after a new baby and her three older children.

How do I know all of this? After years of searching (my adoption was never talked about with my adopted family, and my adoptive mother—an adoptee herself—threw all my records away), I have strong memories of discovering a box and reading through some of the records and telling people I had been born in a hut. Somehow I realised, or was told, that the records would still be held by the council who organised my adoption. And despite a big fire at the offices, I was lucky. My records survived.

One day—just now, I can't remember when, maybe in my early forties?—I was given a huge file which contained a birth certificate, my mother's statement, detailed records from the orphanage. Details of the arguments between Hong Kong Social Services and all the agencies involved that went on over years when my parents could not adopt me because my mother had not cited them as specific adopters on her consent. And British law demanded that Hong Kong Social Services go back and find her to ask for her specific consent. That itself is a story I'd like to know more about. Did they? How long did they spend searching? Where did they look? Who did they ask, and what constitutes a proper search? I guess I'll never know the answers to these questions.

Since they couldn't find my mother, I was made a ward of court, and a Guardian ad Litem was appointed for me, who consented to my adoption, after Hong Kong Social Services reported that they had failed to locate her.

I never wrote this stuff down before. I have talked about it, tried to make sense of it—to explain how, despite all, how lucky I feel. So much luck, in being relinquished with a story, rather than abandoned in a stairwell with no name or birth certificate. Out of the blue, when I was in my forties, I discovered that 100 of us—yes, 100—were brought over as part of a British Government project in the 1960s. International Year of the Refugee. Lots of refugees from Hong Kong brought to the UK on BOAC (now British Airways), with Dr Barnardo's or NCH acting as intermediaries. And of those 100, just three of us were relinquished. Just three had a past and a story. Something to go on. Something that might help tie us back to our past, in our future, should we so wish.

And I think I always wished it. Wanted to see faces that echoed back to me. Whispered to me, "you belong to me, to here, to us. You are one of us."

And now I see the echoing and the life-affirming looks. Now I see this in my own dear children, in my little part-Chinese granddaughter Phoebe. I have three people who share my genes. Amazing.

And there's part of me that thinks: three? Surely that should be enough. I revel in the knowingness of this trio. But I want to find out for them and for me. I want to find out more. I want to tread on the soil of the place, of the hut where I was born. And though I know it's unlikely I will find my mother, I would like to see an image of her. A photograph. Or hear a story from someone who knew her.

So, I've started. I've come from St Ives in Cornwall, with a biggish suitcase of stuff that I've now whittled down to the bare minimum. Life is better with less stuff. Less is more with regards to stuff—but not with regards to family?

I drove myself from Cornwall up to the Midlands. It doesn't sound like much, but this is no mean feat for a girl who has done car pirouettes on the M5 and lived to tell the tale. I take this as a sign that someone is looking out for me, wants me to stay alive—I still have a lot to do.

Finally, after the first leg of a long journey, here I am. In this strange and eerily deserted Birmingham Airport. A massive shopping centre full of unnecessary stuff, all lit up with fluorescent light screaming, "Feel better, buy me, buy me." I want to feel better, and I am tempted to buy a little something to calm me down. But I come to my senses and resist. I'm travelling ninja light. Me and my phone, and my keyboard. Me and my hopes and my dreams.

I can see Victoria's Secret shop and Boots, and Costa, and Wetherspoons, and Home of the Whopper. Giraffe. And just a few people, all on a journey to somewhere.

There are Christmas lights, all in red and green, and big words made to look like handwriting, fashioned in pink neon that I can't quite make out. Easing me in for a destination where I won't be able to understand or write a word. I'm breathing it all in deeply. Ready and happy and scared and not ready, to leave all of this behind. Content, quietly excited, but quietly questioning my sanity. Ready, almost ready, for the next part of my journey.

*The Po Leung Kuk, founded in 1878 as the Society for the Protection of Women and Children, is a charitable organisation in Hong Kong that, 144 years later, still provides support for orphaned children, education and other services including care for the elderly.

Like the Three Wise Monkeys in Transit

November 15 2018
Flight A188 to Hong Kong

A twelve-hour flight from Charles de Gaulle to Hong Kong. I'm squished between two older Chinese men. I've no idea how old they are, and for the first time I understand why people struggle to guess my age. The guesses I get swing wildly—from the flattering "not a day over 40" to the sobering "late 60s?" But I digress.

Both men wear baseball caps. The one by the window is distinguishable by the grey hair escaping from under his. He stares out the window for the entire flight, ignoring cabin crew requests to stop opening the blind and flooding the dark cabin with light. He watches nothing on the in-flight screen except the flight path. Occasionally, he pulls a crumpled dinner invitation from his pocket and inspects it—a typed-out menu. Oddly, he becomes my in-flight entertainment, though not in a good way.

On my other side, in the aisle seat, the man sings to himself and fiddles with a Rubik's cube. Click-click, sing-sing. Click-click, sing-sing.

And I'm stuck in the middle, wearing a Jack Wills onesie with buttons that won't quite do up, revealing more than I'd like. I imagine I look more like a weary Chinese woman in her late 60s than the sleek, forty-something version I wish I was. I'm acutely aware of how underdressed I am, sandwiched between my fellow travellers. I've got a silk nightie on underneath, but the straps won't stay up. A dressing gown or coat would have helped. I have neither.

They, of course, are amply clothed. Window man wears a grey Nike hooded anorak. Rubik's Cube man sports a beige, multi-pocketed fishing-style waistcoat.

What a strange trio we make. I start to fantasise—maybe, against all odds, we're related. It's the sort of thing non-Asians say: "Well, they all look the same." We certainly share matching eye bags. All looking and acting a little odd.

I want to strike up a conversation, but I don't dare. I've already had an awkward moment with the air hostess, who tried to speak to me first in Cantonese, then Mandarin. I said, "I'm English," and got *that* look—bemused, confused. It turned to mild panic when she couldn't find my pre-ordered vegetarian meal. Only beef and noodles or chicken and rice remained. I took both, gave the meat to the men (they smiled), and made do with a rice-and-noodle supper.

If I can't explain myself to the air hostess or chat to my flight buddies, what hope is there in my so-called homeland, full of people who are like me but not at all like me? Part of me wonders if this is all a big mistake.

But we're beginning our descent. I'm told to stow my hand baggage. I'm told Hong Kong is a no-smoking terminal. I'm mistakenly passed over when they hand out immigration cards. I'm told to collect all my baggage from carousel number 5.

The irony of that instruction hits me much later. If only *that* were all the baggage I was bringing home. The emotional weight I've carried for years is already rising to the surface—the old, familiar ache of belonging and not belonging. Of being, and not being, Chinese. Baggage I'd far rather leave circling carousel number 5.

Afternote:

As we landed, the "look out the window" man suddenly began an earnest conversation in broken English. He lives in Edinburgh, a retired restaurateur, returning to Hong Kong to get his ID card and visit his brothers. His wife is flying out on Saturday.

He asks a lot of questions, but struggles with the concept of being born and then adopted. He doesn't know where Cornwall is. I struggle to understand his accent—despite his 48 years in Edinburgh.

He keeps repeating the one Mandarin phrase I know well: "太贵了 *Tài guìle*"—"Too expensive." Houses, food, cars—*everything* in Hong Kong.

So, the only other phrase I've mastered—"Do you have anything cheaper?"—may soon come in handy.

Seeking Long Lost Family and My Recently Lost Luggage

I've arrived. But my two small pieces of luggage have not.

Close friends and family know I'm always losing my stuff—it's become a bit of a joke. Losing a beanie or gloves doesn't matter too much, but losing important things like wedding rings, wallets, keys, or crucial documents? That's another matter.

When I arrived early at Birmingham Airport, I thought it best to check both pieces of luggage. That way, I couldn't lose anything. One case contained all my valuable, hard-earned root-tracing documents, along with a duplicate set I'd made on Martin's advice. What an idiot. How could I get it so wrong? What was I thinking?

On landing, I turned on my phone and was greeted with this text:

Flight AF188: your baggage item no. 102196 will not be delivered upon arrival. It is still in transport. Please go to the Air France Baggage Services desk. Then another text for my other bag—a small rucksack with the few clothes I brought: mainly pyjamas, socks, and underwear.

What followed was an hour of trailing around and trying to communicate with officials. I looked like crap in my Jack Wills onesie. Everyone else—speaking fluent Cantonese or Mandarin (I can't tell which)—was dressed in navy and sleek business black, or expensive Burberry and other designer gear. I was tired and emotional, with no chance of dressing for the kind of conversations I needed to have. Like the one I was now struggling through: trying to get Air France to start tracing my luggage immediately rather than the "week to ten days" they were proposing.

At home, I have a dedicated outfit for difficult conversations: a tailored navy Paul Smith suit and a cashmere rollneck that perfectly matches the fleck in the design. I call it my "don't f**k with me" gear. I wish I had that suit now. I wish even more that I could speak Cantonese.

If I were talking to someone whose first language was English, they'd pick up on my urgency—my frustration. But the young agent I'm speaking to (who looks about twelve) doesn't pick up on any of it. He seems to think that since I'm staying for three months, it's all ever-so-slightly funny and fine. He guesses my bags might arrive tomorrow at midnight. Or next week.

I haven't felt this disempowered—or this delegitimised—in a long time.

I can hear you sighing. Not so much in sympathy, but aghast at my stupidity. I know, I know. But I wanted to travel light.

It occurs to me that I'm coming "home" with about the same amount of stuff I left with back in 1962. Today, it's just me, my handbag, and my comfort toy—a stuffed monkey called Marve.

Back then, it was just me, my little bag, and a blow-up Father Christmas.

Roomies

November 16 2018 10.30am

Hop Inn Mody Hostel, Hong Kong. 8 bed dorm

Arriving in Hong Kong at night and trying to find Hop Inn Mody was far from the exciting, neon-lit experience I'd imagined. The lights of Kowloon dazzled—but in a disorienting way. I wandered up and down Mody Road, desperate and confused, unable to find the hostel's hidden entrance.

When I finally did, the lift was out of order. A small blessing, I had no luggage to carry after the baggage fiasco. But the cracked walls, greasy stairs, and cloths draped on bamboo racks on every landing were not the red carpet welcome I'd secretly dreamed of.

I was hungry, but too anxious to stray far from the hostel. I found a small café and, despite a huge English menu, ordered the safest thing I could see—prawn fried rice. Not exactly a bold culinary adventure, but I needed comfort more than risk.

This wasn't the homecoming I'd imagined. But this journey isn't about glamour. It's about heritage, roots, reckoning. Still, this start wasn't exactly blog-worthy.

The next part of my blog I wrote with Paloma in mind. Paloma is my dear friend from St Ives, ten years older and much more tolerant than me. We once shared a room in Faro, Portugal, where she patiently endured my mess, my middle-of-the-night antics (me showing her pictures of baby hedgehogs at 2am). We survived a week's holiday together, and we're still close. Whether she'd ever room with me again is another question. Paloma calls me her roomie and I call her roomie too.

Paloma, meet my new roomies—all seven of them.

Four metal bunk beds. Windowless room. I've got a bottom bunk, and what few possessions I have are padlocked in a wire cage underneath.

When someone rummages in theirs, a loud clanking fills the room, followed by scraping metal as locks are wrangled shut.

Right now, though, there's silence—except the sound of a running shower. It's been going since 9am. I think I've been silently relegated to last in line.

I catch glimpses of my roomies but don't dare stare. They're all Asian, all with long, thick black hair that makes mine feel thin and inadequate. My thoughts, shallow and fleeting, bullet themselves out:

- All so young
- So intent on beautifying
- Hard not to stare
- (Uncomfortably) imagine the opening number of *Miss Saigon*
- Straighteners? In a hostel?
- Curlers in fringes—like a shampoo and set
- White face masks, geisha-like
- Make-up palettes, contouring, false lashes
- Suitcases full of beauty products
- No rucksacks in sight
- Push-up bras, tiny skirts, "I'm a flower girl" t-shirts
- Cheap plastic heels
- So hard not to stare

Finally, I get my turn in the shower. It's a long, non-eco-friendly drench. I've blown my daily food budget hiring a towel, but it's worth it.

I emerge. The ritual continues—silent, methodical. It's like watching a slow-motion religious ceremony.

I get dressed:

- Knot the straps of my silk nightie to make it more chaste
- Pull on the bottom half of my Jack Wills onesie
- Tie the top half and hood around my waist
- Strategically wrap a black cashmere jumper for modesty
- Add a headscarf—not Queen-style, more Alicia Keys (I hope)

- A dab of red lipstick
- Day-old socks
- Big black Vivo barefoot shoes

The shoes aren't pretty, but they're necessary. My feet—misshapen and aching—need support. I wonder if my mother's feet were bound. My grandmother's? Do my new roomies care for their feet? They don't appear to be in the least bit concerned. Perhaps they will, when they're older. It was only recently that someone told me that my soul resides in the soles of my feet.

Five minutes of philosophical musing, and I'm ready—me and my "I've seen life" liver-spotted face. Last time I was in Hong Kong, eager sales assistants pushed whitening products into my hands when I was simply wanting to buy toothpaste. The potions promised a younger, whiter and brighter complexion and the main ingredient was lambs' placenta.

I couldn't explain then—and still can't—that I don't eat meat and neither would I ever dream of smothering my face in a lambs' placenta. I don't eat meat! Another phrase I must add to my useful Mandarin phrase list.

Still, they say beauty is in the eye of the beholder. To calm and soothe myself, I repeat quietly to myself *I am beautiful. I am beautiful. I am beautiful.*

No, I haven't prepped and preened like my new roomies, but I'm ready to swim in this fast, unpredictable Hong Kong current.

Which is just as well—because at 09:30 sharp, Winnie Siu Davies arrives, armed with emergency clothes and ready to begin our search.

A Bit About Winnie

When you're about to embark on a mythical quest—especially one to find your birth family in the city of your origin—you need a guide. A magical helper. The kind of character who turns up early in the film, says something cryptic or wise, and then becomes the person who'll walk beside you when things get rough. Think Jiminy Cricket, Pumbaa, or Mushu... only in real life. That's Winnie.

This isn't an official blog entry, but I want to tell you about Winnie Siu Davies, because understanding her helps make sense of everything that follows.

Long Lost Family contacted Winnie when they took up my case, and they passed her details to me when they closed it. She played a pivotal role in convincing me I had a better chance of finding my birth family by coming to Hong Kong. She even helped me choose the hostel for my first month's stay.

I hope Winnie forgave my state when she turned up at 9:30am, the morning after my overnight flight. I had wanted to make a good first impression, but after a jet-lagged, restless night in a dorm full of strangers and the stress of lost luggage, I must have looked a wreck. Winnie said nothing about my appearance or foggy brain—but she had plenty to say about my missing birth records. I can't put her words in writing!

You don't want to get on the wrong side of Winnie. She's strong, opinionated, belligerent, and argumentative. She reminds me of myself—only with a sharper edge and a skillset that far surpasses mine. And she is also one of the kindest people on this planet. She gives her time freely—not for money or praise—but because she believes it's the right thing to do.

If you're lucky enough to have Winnie on your side as you search for a birth family in Hong Kong, you've got the best ally possible in a city-sized haystack.

Winnie is a sculptor, artist, and teacher. Outside of her full-time job, she devotes all her spare hours to helping adoptees like me trace their roots. More recently, she's taken on the additional challenge of supporting young mothers searching for the babies they were forced to give up. She's had many successes, and she runs the website look4mama.com. Her connections with Hong Kong media are invaluable—radio, TV, and newspapers regularly feature her searches and success stories. Most nights, Winnie is still up at 4am, poring over records, decoding riddles, calling strangers, and helping adoptees and mothers around the world. She does it all for free.

This was the woman who greeted me that first morning, carrying a bundle of spare clothes. They weren't my size or style, but I pounced on them like they were haute couture.

Winnie, my mentor and friend, stayed by my side throughout my search in Hong Kong. I still can't believe how lucky I was to be introduced to someone with such deep experience of Hong Kong bureaucracy, fluent in both English and Cantonese, and with such a determined, generous spirit.

Here's my own entry on Winnie's website, look4mama.com—one of hundreds of appeals for help that she has posted. I guess, like me, you wish you could read Mandarin:

女嬰 1960 年 10 月 20 日出生

(生母: 賴蘇金 1997 年過身**)**

現欲尋: **生父: 黃添 (曾住元朗、上水、大埔)**

生母被生父離棄後患腎病在院期間未能照顧初生女玉蘭,

而被迫將初生女送入保良局。

之後女兒玉蘭被送去英國夫婦收養。

玉蘭專程由英國回港尋親生父。

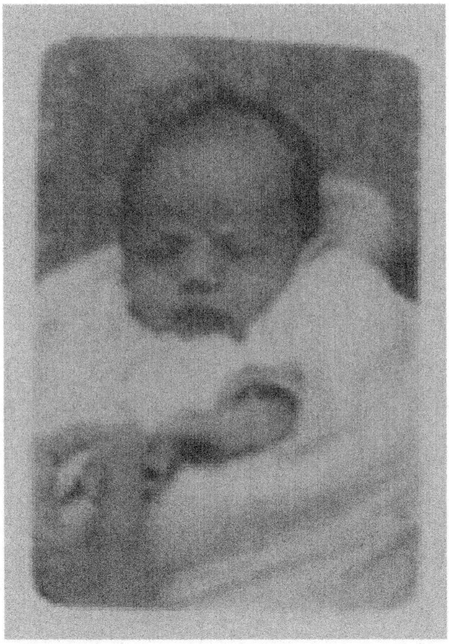

Following in Her Footsteps

November 17, 2018
Kam Shan Village

In the statutory declaration explaining why she gave me up for adoption, my mother listed her address as an unmarked hut in Melon Garden, Kam Shan Village, Tai Po.

Winnie cleverly managed to get us to the village by persuading a helpful estate agent to take us there. We agreed to justify her journey by viewing a nearby apartment that was up for rental. To our surprise, Kam Shan Village was still there, right on the fringes of Tai Po, mostly hidden behind layers of redevelopment. A small residential area consisting of low, weathered houses, footpaths narrowed by pot plants and laundry racks, dilapidated unoccupied huts, and the occasional bark of a dog behind a rusted gate. We wandered through the village, taking in the few huts that remain. Winnie explained that the right to inhabit them is likely passed down through generations. When I learned the going rate for the apartment we were "viewing" (£1.2k a month for a rundown two-bedroom flat), it struck me how something so modest could carry such weight—far more secure and valuable than the apartment we were pretending to view.

It's hard to take in: I might be walking, standing, breathing in the very place my mother once stood.

We've decided to return, this time with posters and letters in hand, hoping to find someone who remembers the village as it was in the 1960s. I've already posted in a Facebook group called Hong Kong in the 1960s. Around fifty people have responded—sending well wishes and resharing my search across other platforms.

This post may not be the most eloquent. But I promised myself I'd blog daily. I'm still trying to navigate this place. One moment, I'm in the chaotic streets near my hostel, nearly trampled by shoppers. The area is lined with designer outlets and luxury malls that contain restaurants, hotels, spas, cinemas—even ice rinks. MTR stations open directly into these malls, making it nearly impossible to exit without being drawn into the shimmer of window displays.

If you can resist the pull of branded glamour, the night markets aren't far. These stalls brim with near-perfect knock-offs: Gucci, Chanel, Louis Vuitton. Visitors from China flock here to buy luxury fakes by the bagful. The counterfeits are so convincing that someone like me—uninitiated—would struggle to spot the difference.

And then, just a few stops down the MTR line from this world of glitz and imitation, I find myself staring at a hut—cobbled together with wood, corrugated metal, cardboard, and tarpaulin. A hut that might be like the one my mother once lived in.

It's Here

November 17 2018 at what feels like the middle of the night
Hop Inn Mody Hostel, Hong Kong. 8 bed dorm

The girl on reception knocked on the dorm door, interrupting my fragile attempts at sleep. I crawled out from my bunk, annoyed and groggy—but also slightly thrilled. I had a feeling I knew why I was being called.

My suitcase had finally arrived.

After 48 hours of anxiety, uncertainty, and lost sleep, it was here—along with all my precious root-tracing documents, safe and intact. The man who delivered it is my hero. I wanted to hug him, but somehow managed to restrain myself.

I'm now grinning from ear to ear as I write this, caught in that strange mix of frustration with Air France and immense gratitude that they actually pulled through.

Winnie will be overjoyed when she hears the news.

Air France. Your advertising tells me "Elegance is a journey" Try telling that to the woman stranded in a Jack Wills onesie, living off duty-free Toblerone because you lost all her luggage. But thank you for finding and returning it. I adore you. And I salute you.

Fitting In

November 18 2018
The streets of Kowloon

Yesterday, I wandered the streets of Kowloon with no plan, no schedule—just open to what the day would bring.

I've visited Hong Kong before, as a tourist in my twenties. But this time felt different. I moved freely, without an agenda. Everything felt both new and strangely familiar. It was comforting. Like something here recognises me—even if I never find my birth family.

One of the first things I noticed was the number of people exercising in public: tai chi, stretching, dancing. Everywhere. By poolside railings, in parks, in quiet corners of the city. Many parks even had little gym areas built in. I watched groups of Filipino maids dancing together to loud music, laughing, full of energy.

There was something joyful and unselfconscious about it all—movement as celebration, not performance.

It struck me how normal it is here to use public space this way. In St Ives, when I stretch my legs on railings like a makeshift ballet barre, people look at me like I'm from another planet.

I also came across an enormous public pool in Kowloon Park—clean, busy, and buzzing with people of all ages and abilities. There was a diving pool, a children's pool, a pool for the elderly and disabled, lanes for swimmers, and a general splash-around pool for the rest.

Some people stretched solemnly by the pool's edge. Others danced in the water or floated quietly. It reminded me of swimming in Cornwall—though only when no one is watching.

Later, above the shopfront of my favourite Hong Kong designer, Shanghai Tang, I spotted a huge backlit poster. Two young Chinese models posed in designer knitwear—bold jumpers made from colourful crocheted granny squares.

By coincidence, I'd just learned how to crochet a granny square before coming out here. I'd even packed a hook and some wool. It felt like a tiny thread from home, tugging gently across the distance.

Role Reversal

November 18 2018 noon
The Peninsula Hotel

Today I met up with my friend Liz. Like me, she lives in St Ives, Cornwall—only she's Cornish through and through, not an *emmet* (Cornish for someone who's moved there) like me. She's been in Hong Kong since July. And, just like me, she's recently become a grandmother.

But there's a twist: her daughter and granddaughter are here in Hong Kong, while my little family is back in the middle of England. It's a role reversal of sorts. My quarter-Chinese granddaughter, Phoebe, was born in England. Liz's 100% Cornish granddaughter was born here, in Hong Kong.

I spot Liz in the crowd at the Peninsula fountains, a popular meeting spot just outside the iconic 5-star hotel, known for its majestic entrance and fleet of Peninsula-green Rolls-Royces. She's scanning the crowd for me, but today everything feels back to front. I'm close enough to touch her before she sees me.

Startled, she laughs. "Normally I can spot you in an instant, Laura," she says. "But here, you're just one in seven million." I know what she means—but it hits differently. The task of finding my birth family in this city of lookalikes suddenly feels impossibly huge.

Liz is one of the liveliest people I know—a singer, a yogi, a guiding light. Today she stands out effortlessly in Tsim Sha Tsui. Tall, willowy, blonde, her style a mix of designer, vintage, and high street. Some of the ultra-wealthy, yet questionably dressed women here (think head-to-toe Burberry, no variation) could take a few notes from Liz.

We walk through the designer baby mall and catch up. The baby changing rooms are pure luxury: dim lighting, stainless steel counters, and plush seating for nursing mothers. I can't help thinking of my daughter-in-law back home, trying to change Phoebe on a cracked, plastic pull-down in a dingy toilet cubicle.

We marvel at Baby Burberry, Baby Armani, Baby D&G. Who pays these prices? Who spends £3,000 on a designer pram?

Later, we drift through the Ocean Terminal supermarket—more food gallery than grocer. Grapes are £26. An onion is £3. Sweet potatoes, surprisingly, are a bargain at £4 apiece. We laugh—Liz's husband used to run Trims, the fruit and veg shop back in St Ives.

Here, a small mortgage might just cover the cost of cheddar or a pint of milk. Except, that is, for Cornish clotted cream. At just under £4, it's a total steal.

In Cornwall, we say "When in Rome…" and reach for the jam and scones.

But in Hong Kong?

Skip the cream tea.

Pass the fishball noodles. A bowl costs less than one plain scone.

Coming Soon

November 19 2018 23.03

Hop Inn Mody Hostel, Hong Kong. 8 bed dorm

I am up far too late, and I have so many things I want to say. But it's 23:03 on Monday night, and I really need to sleep.

So instead of a proper blog entry, here's a list.

Today I've learned:

- Why I was obsessed with Paddington Bear
- Why being married to a Liam Neeson-type from *Taken* isn't as brilliant as it sounds
- That learning to navigate is like anything else—it takes practice, patience, and baby steps
- Why I love Kowloon Park swimming pool and the Peninsula Hotel—and why I'm not so fond of the Harbour Spa in St Ives anymore
- That I don't need to take my Octopus card out of my phone holder every time I use it—it works like a ski pass. I feel stupid for not knowing, but now I do. I feel smug
- How to get around on the MTR. Sort of
- That Jehovah's Witnesses might be onto something. And also onto nothing
- That lots of people want to move to Hong Kong, but you need to apply *to apply*. No, really
- That a vegetarian aubergine and rice dish can come with unexpected (and unwelcome) pork bits
- Why the doorman to this building always looks so happy
- Why being placed in Po Leung Kuk orphanage, as opposed to others, might matter
- And loads of other things

Let's talk more tomorrow.

Oh—and a small favour. If you're following this blog and like any of my posts, please click the *like* button. It helps to know you're out there. It comforts me, here in my little Hong Kong cell.

Thank you. x

I Realise Jehovah's Witnesses (JWs) Are Somewhat Wise, Maybe

November 20 2018 10.30am
Hop Inn Mody Hostel, Hong Kong. 8 bed dorm

I'm starting to think Jehovah's Witnesses (JWs) might be onto something.

I must have looked sad—or maybe just a little lost—the other day, because a JW thrust a leaflet into my unreceptive hands titled *Help for Those Who Grieve*. In the UK, I would've handed it straight back and politely declined. But here in Hong Kong, I'm too scared to even attempt a bit of Putonghua—no one understands me anyway. If I try out a couple of barely comprehensible words like "hello" or "thank you," the reply comes in a torrent of Mandarin I can't follow. So instead, I resort to slow, broken English to explain why I can't speak Chinese. It's a tortuous process I now avoid at all costs.

One day, I must tell you the story of my first visit to Hong Kong. My new Chinese friend had invited me to her home, but when her mother opened the door and saw me and my tall British husband standing there, she slammed it shut in our faces. She thought we were Jehovah's Witnesses. A memorable first impression.

Over the years, I've politely closed the door on many JWs myself—though never quite like my adoptive mother, Cath, who taught me to slam it hard from a young age, and not just to JWs. I've since modified that particular lesson.

Still, I have to admit the advice in that leaflet is surprisingly sound. And having something in English to read was an unexpected comfort—especially once I learned to mentally replace the word *God* with something that made more sense to me. Reading it made me pause and reflect on why I'm really here.

No, dear JWs, I'm not grieving in the traditional sense—no one has died—but all twelve suggestions felt appropriate to help me navigate this foreign city and this strange search:

1. **Accept support from family and friends.** I'm a bit short on both out here, so please send virtual support (see request at the end of the previous post).
2. **Watch your diet and make time for exercise.** So—less dim sum, more swimming.
3. **Get plenty of sleep.** No more 2 AM WhatsApp chats. And my blog will be finished by 11 PM at the latest.
4. **Be flexible.** Absolutely essential when you're living in an 8-bed dorm. Both emotional and physical flexibility required—especially when all your belongings live in a giant wire cage under a lower bunk.
5. **Avoid self-destructive habits.** I think I'm okay here… though I still bite my left thumbnail when I'm stressed.
6. **Balance your time.** I need to do more and worry less about keeping everyone updated on my search.
7. **Keep a routine.** Struggling. Yesterday, I didn't eat until 4 PM and didn't sleep until 4 AM.
8. **Avoid making big decisions too soon.** Like whether I should disappear to Vietnam for two or three weeks over Christmas…
9. **Remember your loved one(s).** I think they mean someone who's died. I've got no shortage of absent and much-missed family and friends on my mind. Hence the 2 AM conversations—calling from the hostel common room so as not to wake my dorm mates.
10. **Get away.** Check. Done that.

11. **Help others.** I wish there was someone here I could help. I suppose I can help strangers—as long as they're not asking for directions in Cantonese.
12. **Re-evaluate your priorities.** Yes. Always. I'm pretty good at checking whether my ladder's leaning against the right wall before I start climbing it.

So—with points 3, 6, and 7 especially in mind—it's goodnight from me, and goodnight from the good ol' JWs.

The Happy Concierge

November 21 2018
Hop Inn Mody Hostel, Hong Kong.

Many people come and go in this building because it isn't just the Hop Inn Mody Hostel. Hidden behind a narrow, dimly lit entrance that's easy to miss, it's something of an Aladdin's cave. Alongside my hostel, there's a restaurant, a tailor, other guesthouses and hostels, and businesses I haven't yet figured out.

The whole building is guarded by uniformed men who take turns monitoring the CCTV 24/7 from behind a tiny glass window in a room that wouldn't look out of place in a prison. They also spring into action when the lifts break down—directing frustrated visitors to the back stairwell, which is poorly lit and cluttered with bamboo poles hung with what I can only assume is clean laundry. It all looks quite dirty to me.

Most of the guards wear scowls and don't return a smile, even if you try. But there is one who is always cheerful and friendly.

Today, I discovered why.

He has YouTube karaoke playing all the time, and today I heard him singing along—in perfect English. He's good. His standout performance? Elvis's version of *My Way*.

This evening, I joined in.

I think it might just become my anthem for the search.

The Liam Neeson/Paddington Bear Stuff

November 21 2018 09.00

Tai Wo Plaza, Hong Kong.

Transcription from notes made at Tai Wo Plaza, the nearest MTR station to my birth mother's village. I was waiting to meet some of Winnie's press contacts: an Apple News reporter/photographer and the HK01 news team.

I did it. I made it from my hostel to the nearest MTR station to Kam Shan Village, where my birth mother once lived. My face was beaming—I'd navigated here solo, waking at 7:00am, showered, left with plenty of time. I didn't get lost. I got off at the right station. I boarded the right line.

"So? And?" sneers my inner critic. But not today. Today, I won't let that voice dampen my joy. I sketch tiny balloons and write: *She did it.*

Because I am that same girl who once spent two hours trying to find her way back to the family tent. The girl who thought the coloured grab rails on the London Underground indicated the line she was on—with disastrous consequences. The mother whose children still factor in double time for any journey. The one whose twelve-year-old daughter once navigated them both off the Picos de Europa mountains in Spain. The woman who can't read ski lift maps and once had to sidestep up a steep mountain because she got stuck at the top after the lifts closed.

One of my earliest memories is being lost at the end of my own street—small, confused, scared—head swinging left and right like I was watching a tennis match, having no idea which way was home.

LOST. Always lost. Or terrified of getting lost.

My work in Warwickshire schools was the same: even in buildings I'd been to dozens of times, I couldn't find my way from the staff room to the classroom. Always anxious. Always hoping I'd arrive where I was supposed to be.

Even in St Ives, two months in, I still couldn't get to the Tate without straying down a blind alley.

But today, in a foreign country—*the* country I was born in—I am exactly where I need to be. I got here an hour early. I ate dim sum with a Chinese man sporting the worst comb-over I've ever seen. He had a full breakfast; I had two tiny dumplings. I wonder if his heart is full of joy too, or if he's just wondering why his hair-restoring shampoo isn't working.

Liam Neeson.

Remember I said I was married to someone like Liam Neeson in Taken? Not in looks—Martin doesn't resemble Liam—but in the way he acts. In Taken 2, Liam's character is blindfolded, shoved into a truck, and taken to a bad guy's hideout. Turkey maybe? I forget. He manages to call his wife and, based on the sounds he heard while blindfolded, how long he was in the truck, and the wind direction, he figures out exactly where he is. Implausible, yes. Also: how does he still have a phone?

Anyway—Martin is like that. He once navigated his way back to a hotel in Oman on day one of a business trip. Forgot the name, had no business card, no location written down. He even rang to ask me for help. Me! Like the blind leading the blind.

Martin knows how to use a compass properly. I think he *is* a compass. I call him Pembo Nav. Pembo Nav never fails.

But being married to Pembo Nav has a downside. Because he was so capable, I never *had* to develop my own skills. I became more helpless with each passing year. Just as he relied on my cooking, I relied on his navigation. Before I left for Hong Kong, we had a brief conversation about using the Remoska cooker to make healthy food. We figured fish and chips, pizza, and full English breakfasts might lose their appeal after a week.

This time apart might be good for both of us.

I came here to find my birth mother. But maybe—just maybe—I'm finding myself.

Footnote: Paddington Bear

When I was a teenager, I wrote to *Jim'll Fix It* and asked to be dressed up as Paddington Bear. I know, I know—weird. But as it turns out, *he* was the weird one. I got off lightly—he never replied.

I loved Paddington. I even bought a red duffle coat. Never really knew why. Then the other day it hit me: Paddington was a foreign bear, lost in a strange country, with a small suitcase and a label asking somebody—anybody—to look after him.

When I arrived at London Heathrow, I was met by my adoptive family. They might have even come via Paddington Station. I was 15 months old, dressed in a white fur coat, with just one small BOAC bag. No visible label—but I didn't need one. I was desperate for someone to look after me.

Funny how the dots eventually join up...

Not Your Average Tourist

November 22 2018 21.00
Hop Inn Mody Hostel, Hong Kong. In bed in the 8 bed dorm

Sometimes you have to stop searching to start discovering. After days of chasing elusive needles in unfathomable haystacks—names, records, ghosts of the past—today I decided to down tools and be a tourist. But not your average one. No Disneyland, no Peak Tram queues or overpriced attractions. I wanted a different Hong Kong. One that didn't feel manufactured.

So I left the polished madness of Tsim Sha Tsui and took the MTR to Sham Shui Po (SSP)—gritty, arty, alive. It's one of the city's oldest districts, where people still live and work side by side. No sleek glass towers here—just concrete tenement blocks, temples, repurposed buildings draped in bamboo scaffolding. Even the street names are a treasure map: Button Street, Bead Street, Leather Street, Ribbon Street.

The main drag hums with flea markets—especially the second-hand tech kind. Mostly men rummage through battered boxes of tangled chargers, outmoded mobiles, ancient cameras and VHS players. It's all slightly absurd and oddly joyful. SSP buzzes with a different kind of energy—one of locals, not tourists, of possibility in the discarded.

I came here, too, for something more traditional—the joss paper effigy workshop. Down a quiet side street, I found it: stacked paper replicas of things the dead might want in the afterlife. Designer handbags, mobile phones, Ferraris, beloved pets, children's toys. It was poignant, strangely funny, oddly moving. I wondered what my kids might choose for me. A saxophone? A swimming pool? Effigies of my cat Dorey? Hopefully not a Ferrari. I like to think they'd know me well enough not to need a list.

I confess—it wasn't all about flea markets and paper ghosts. I'd planned the day around my love of street food and had my eye on a Michelin-starred dim sum house: Tim Ho Wan. SSP isn't fancy, but it's a street-snacker's paradise. As a solo diner, I got fast-tracked past the queue and seated with a man from New York. We didn't share food, but we did share delight—especially over my har gow dumplings: glistening, pleated, perfect. I savoured them too quickly but lingered over my custard tart, breaking it into four parts like communion. A Michelin-starred lunch for £8—now *that's* a spiritual experience.

After seven hours wandering SSP, my legs ached. I headed to Kowloon Park for a swim—my version of therapy. No frills, but clean, warm, inclusive, open until 10pm, and only a couple of pounds a visit. Elderly swimmers limber up with tai chi. There's no shame in age or disability here—just movement, care, and community. The changing rooms are spotless. Hairdryers double as full-body warmers. People place neat yellow tags on broken equipment, marked "REPAIR," and—imagine this—the items get fixed. Efficiency, accessibility, respect.

It made me think of the Harbour Spa in St Ives, beloved but clunky. There, a broken swimsuit spinner disappears for months. Showers are scalding. The steam room's out of order more often than not. We joke, we moan—but after today, I can't help but wonder why it has to be this way.

That said, there *is* one habit I won't be bringing home: spitting into the poolside drain. Apparently, it's a thing here—and while it's discouraged (and fined), it still happens. Let's just say I'll be sticking to tai chi, not that tradition.

As I lay back in my dorm bed tonight, warm, full, and grateful, I realised: I may not have ticked off the "Top Ten" sights, but I experienced a version of Hong Kong that felt more real, more human. Less spectacle, more texture. Not your average tourist day—and exactly the break I needed.

Hireth

November 23 2018 10.30am

Hop Inn Mody Hostel, Hong Kong. 8 bed dorm

Hireth is a beautiful Cornish word with no direct English translation. It describes a complex, bittersweet feeling—a deep longing for a place, even one you've never known. As I continue my journey to find my family, I'm forging new connections and putting down roots. Yet this morning, waking in my quiet, windowless dorm, I couldn't shake a yearning for St Ives—the magical sky, the soft pink light, and the profound silence of out-of-season Cornwall.

I miss watching the sun rise over the sea from my penthouse balcony, the sky flushed deep red, its glow reflecting off the waves. The stillness of dawn, broken only by the distant cry of gulls, feels a world away from this compact hostel, where silence is heavy—punctuated only when a group of travellers arrives together. They usually speak in languages I don't understand, which somehow deepens the ache of homesickness.

I know I'm lucky to have found this place—my temporary home on the other side of the world, in the very city I once longed for. Yet hireth cuts both ways. As much as I'm pulled toward the promise of finding my roots, part of me still aches for the quiet beauty of Cornwall—for the place that once let me simply be.

Maybe hireth isn't a place at all, but the space between what was and what might still be.

The Universe Looks After Me Again

November 23 2018

Hop Inn Mody Hostel, Hong Kong. 8 bed dorm

I do believe that, given half the chance, the universe wants to look after me—especially if I remember to tell her what I want, and stay open to whatever she then provides. Like when I happen upon the perfect parking space when none were initially apparent. Or when friends I haven't seen for ages suddenly call or show up just as I've been yearning to see them. Or when items I've been hunting for magically appear in skips at the side of the road or in charity shops just around the corner.

I know some people think I'm quite bonkers, but I couldn't care less.

Today was yet another example of the universe having my back. I woke up feeling homesick. Lo and behold, there in my inbox was an unexpected invitation to lunch at the Yacht Club at Marina Cove, Sai Kung, New Territories. The invitation came from someone I didn't know—a stranger who'd reached out through the *Hong Kong in the 60s* Facebook page.

Sai Kung is promoted as an escape from urban high-rise life, with activities reminiscent of Cornwall—hiking, kayaking, boating, snorkelling, and diving. Outdoor pursuits I'd never imagined existed in Hong Kong. But just an hour on the MTR and a couple of bus rides later, I realised how mistaken I was. I travelled up to the peninsula and found myself basking in sunshine, overlooking Marina Cove's private berths filled with luxurious yachts and motorboats. For a moment—sipping chilled white wine and tucking into a generous plate of seafood pasta—I forgot I was in Hong Kong and imagined myself in Padstow or Rock.

If I've discouraged you from visiting Hong Kong, please forgive me. You may not fall in love with everything you see, but without doubt, there will be a place that captures your heart. Hong Kong is a city of contrasts—colonial buildings mingling with skyscrapers, ancient temples tucked between traditional villages. While there are densely populated urban areas, there are also green spaces and coastal gems like Sai Kung that surprise and enchant.

Beyond its physical beauty, Hong Kong is home to kind and generous citizens. Many strangers have offered help with my search and invited me to share meals and drinks, refusing any payment. Most of them reached out through the *Hong Kong in the 1960s* Facebook page, where I shared details of my search and asked if anyone had been near my mother's last known address in 1961. Others are friends of newfound acquaintances.

After lunch, I made my way back to Tsim Sha Tsui. Now that I've almost mastered the MTR, the world truly feels like my oyster—or should I say, my Octopus (card)? I'm filled with a bubbling inner joy, reminiscent of the moment I first realised I could string letters together to form words, and words to form sentences. That sudden realisation that I could read and write.

I was the first child in my infant class to learn, but my precociousness knew no bounds. I boldly wrote "PENSLIS" on the class pencil box and vehemently denied it to my teacher, Mrs Houghton. She must have known it was me, but she didn't shame me. Instead, she kept me in during playtime and gently reminded me to continue my good writing—*but only on paper*.

Those memories rejuvenate me. I feel five years old again.

Can you imagine the pictures and words from your early reading books—whether it was *Dick and Dora*, *Fluff and Nip*, or *Janet and John*—magnified and plastered all over the underground walls, and *being able to make sense of it*? Perhaps then you'll understand where I'm coming from. I stand there, transfixed, staring at the map that shows which entrance is closest to which streets—and there are so many streets near my new home.

Can you envision a small, slightly silly, beaming face looking up in wonder? Can you, do you?

That's the MTR-literate me.

Still learning. Still smiling. Still learning to trust the universe a little more each day.

Nothing Much

November 24 2018

Hop Inn Mody Hostel, Hong Kong. 8 bed dorm

"What have you been doing today?" That's the sort of question one spouse might ask another when one of them has taken off to the bright lights of a city on the other side of the world for three months.

Today, I'm glad I don't have to answer it. Not on Facebook or WhatsApp video, where Martin might catch a flicker of embarrassment as I mumble, "Er... not much." Because truly, there's nothing of substance to report. I haven't hired a junk boat or hiked the Dragon's Back. No harbour cruise, no trip to Lantau Island to see the Big Buddha.

I'm in transition—from tourist to someone who's here for a while. And that's a strange kind of no man's land.

The highlight of my day was making porridge, with bananas and blueberries. The first cooking I've done in over a week. I also brewed ginger, lemon and honey tea, washed my clothes, changed my bed, and sorted my stuff. Then sorted it again. And again.

For someone with so little stuff, I seem to spend an inordinate amount of time tending it—as though each item were a small child or needy pet, like the Tamagotchi virtual pets my children loved in the '90s. I notice how happy each thing makes me as I place it carefully back in its rightful place: the 3B pencils, the little pots of honey and tea, charging cables, and the key fob holding the tiniest photo of Phoebe.

I can't remember the last time I felt joy changing a bedsheet and wrestling with a duvet cover. At home, that task is usually accompanied by whingeing and moaning.

I was never the biggest fan of M. Scott Peck's *The Road Less Travelled*, but one line stayed with me: we must build and tend our base camps if we want to conquer mountains.

Over the years, I think I've got good at that—tending base camps, both literal and metaphorical. Mine are built through meditation, writing, reading, swimming, yoga, playing my saxophone. And yes—sorting my stuff.

No mountains have been climbed today, dear Martin, dear readers. Today was about base camp things. So that tomorrow, I'll be ready to climb.

Hostel living can get claustrophobic, so I headed out briefly to follow up on a saxophone lead. Just one MTR stop away, I found a music shop. I hired an alto sax and asked about group lessons. The teacher didn't think I could join formal classes—three months isn't long enough—but he kindly invited me to one of the informal offshoot groups that stick around after class to play.

Instead of taking the MTR back, I walked home with the sax and stopped off at the pool. Probably a stupid idea. But I knew if I went back to the hostel, I wouldn't come out again.

Carrying a saxophone—even an alto—through crowds of weekend shoppers was no joke. I felt clumsy and conspicuous, lumbering through Hong Kong's national pastime of shopping. At one point, we were packed so tightly I thought of giving up and letting the tide carry me along.

I made it to the pool but hadn't thought about what to do with the sax while I swam. I hoped the security office might take it, but my English request was met with a torrent of Cantonese, head shaking, and wild gesturing.

"You go down, you go down," interrupted a cleaning lady who had clearly clocked my distress. She beckoned me to follow, and I did, down to Level 2—training pool area—wondering what I'd find.

Lo and behold: a bay of human-sized lockers. I could've climbed inside and played the damned sax.

So here I am, doing "nothing much," making a home in Hong Kong. Tending my temporary base camp.

And there's no doubt in my mind—Hong Kong has her indebted daughter well and truly covered. For this, I'm grateful.

How to Go Straight from Work to a Party

November 25 2018

Hop Inn Mody Hostel, Hong Kong. 8 bed dorm

I'm both attracted to and repulsed by articles entitled *"How to Go Straight from Work to a Party."* Topical, I suppose, if a) you have a job, and b) you've been invited to parties. Neither currently applies. And even when they did, I don't recall ever doing any of the things they suggest:

Embrace the fancy flat · Throw on some statement jewellery for after-dark sass · Swap your shirt for a silk pyjama top...

One such article popped up on my phone this morning. I ignored it, of course. But let's say I *did* have the need—now I know exactly how I'd do it.

Like Shreya's grandmother used to.

Shreya is my newest roomie, here from London. Today, I finally crawl out of my bunk around 2pm (yes, yes, I know—I've really nailed that daily routine thing from the Jehovah's Witness pamphlet I mentioned before). My eyes are glued shut with mild conjunctivitis. Maybe the pool wasn't as clean as I thought? Or maybe it's sleeping in a sealed room with air-con blasting all night. Or maybe my once-a-week combo of bananas, blueberries, and lemon ginger tea doesn't quite match the 'five-a-day' immunity-boosting routine I aspire to.

But through my bleary, crusted eyes, I spot an apparition: A gorgeous woman standing in the middle of our dorm, twirling herself into a sari. She's pivoting in one of the rare bits of floor not blocked by bunk beds, metal wire cages, or toe-bashing suitcases lying half-open like traps.

She tells me she's getting ready for a wedding party. My eyes, gummed and sore, try to open wider. I must look a state—creased face, sticky eyelids, staring like a stunned cod—while she looks absolutely radiant.

Shreya doesn't seem fazed. She tells me the sari belonged to her grandmother, an Indian doctor who used to wear it to work, then head straight out to weddings or parties without changing.

She shows me some faint stains on the silk—leftovers from surgical chemicals and hospital clean-up routines.

That's what I call real style.

Social fabric, literally.

Who needs the *Daily Telegraph* telling us how to dress? Fishnet ankle socks? Really?

Sliding Doors Day

November 26 2018
Hop Inn Mody Hostel, Hong Kong.

Sliding Doors. I loved that film. Gwyneth Paltrow at her best, before she went a little weird with her vagina-scented candles. For those who haven't seen it, *Sliding Doors* is a romantic comedy that switches between two storylines—each showing a different path the main character's life might take, depending on whether she catches or misses a train. I had my own version of a *Sliding Doors* day today.

Winnie had arranged for us to go back to where I was born. I got off the MTR at Long Ping Station, thirty minutes from where I'm staying in Hong Kong, and took a ten-minute train ride to my birthplace. The doors slid open, and there it was—my other life. The one I might have lived if my mother had kept me. If she hadn't relinquished me, along with that declaration explaining why she was placing me in Po Leung Kuk orphanage, ten weeks after giving birth.

Remember how I told you she gave birth to me—her fourth child—in a hut in Hung Shui Kiu, Tai Po, New Territories? A hut belonging to a man she cohabited with after my birth father deserted her. Pregnant, already with three children, and now left behind. It feels so unjust. A heartbreaking story of someone I might, under different circumstances, have had the chance to know. A woman—my mother—dependent on men to keep her and her children from starvation. A woman who was left, not once, but twice.

That could have been my life: relying on unreliable men. A life marked by poverty, desperation, and illness. I am extremely short-sighted—minus 16.5 in one eye, minus 15.75 in the other. Without glasses or contact lenses, the world dissolves into a blur of unintelligible shapes. My feet, according to the orthopaedic surgeon who saw me when

I was 32, are "the worst and flattest deformed feet I've ever seen." By then, I had done everything I could to straighten them. My baby teeth and gums were in poor shape when I arrived in the UK. But thanks to early NHS dentistry, I now flash pearly whites and healthy pink gums when I smile.

I had the best education—won a scholarship to one of the UK's finest schools for girls. Had I not been adopted; I would have had none of this. I might not even be alive. My life might have mirrored that of many poor elderly Chinese women—illiterate, struggling with their health, barely surviving by collecting cardboard from the streets to supplement their meagre pensions.

People often say, "You must be really angry with her—for giving you up." But as a therapist, I was taught never to say *You must* followed by a feeling. If the assumption is wrong, it shuts the other person down. It's better to say, "I wonder if you feel..." or "I imagine you might feel..."—to be tentative, to invite the truth.

I know now not to be silenced by these assumptions. I can say how it really is for me.

And here's the truth. I'm not angry with my birth mother. I'm angrier at the men who left her, and at the absence of any meaningful social welfare system to support her—or the thousands of refugees who poured into Hong Kong in the 1960s. I feel sorrow for her. I want to cry when I think of what she must have endured. Giving away her ten-week-old baby. Giving birth in the hut of a man who wasn't the child's father, then listing that man's name on the birth certificate because she'd been deserted.

How can I be angry at that?

If I could, I'd tell her: I turned out fine. More than fine.

That I have loved, and am loved in return.

That I have my own family. That she has grandchildren—and now, a great-granddaughter.

I am grateful. Grateful that she relinquished me with a name and a story, rather than abandoning me anonymously.

Of the 103 adoptees brought to England in the 1960s, only three of us have any family information. Most were left in stairwells, on doorsteps, or in public places—babies, left with the hope that someone might find and care for them when their mothers could not. My mother could have done the same. But she didn't.

If I don't find anyone, there will be sadness. Disappointment. But the blows will be softer. Easier to bear. I came home. I stood my ground in this city I'm beginning to call home. I tried.

It's hard to describe the impact of walking through my birthplace. To finally stand in places I've only ever known as unpronounceable names on paper.

To say aloud—in the place she gave birth to me—"Mama, I love you. And I thank you."

Let the words fly to her in the wind.

妈妈(māma), one of the many ways to say mother in Chinese

Lots of huts are still there. The kind my mother might have lived in.

Me with detective Winnie

Do What You Love, However Bad You Are

November 27 2018
Hop Inn Mody Hostel, Hong Kong.

It's Sunday, and I talk to my little family back home—Tom, Lisa, and baby Phoebe. Heavy rain drives everyone into the common room, where a group of Korean women is rustling up a delicious-smelling feast, despite the limited kitchen facilities. Most seats are taken, so I perch on the sofa next to a young guy. He can hear everything I'm saying, but this is the best spot for a decent signal, so I babble on regardless.

I'm completely absorbed, watching my granddaughter wriggle with delight on my phone screen. I'm telling Tom and Lisa about the borrowed saxophone and why it's important for me to keep playing—to maintain my embouchure and diaphragmatic breathing. I explain how happy I am to have the chance to play again, though quite where or how, I haven't yet figured out.

After the call, I turn to the guy on the sofa—to apologise, at least, for subjecting him to my repetitive squawks of "Hello Phoebe! It's nai nai!" He introduces himself. Cody. From LA. A music producer.

He couldn't help overhearing. And then—this: he majored in saxophone at university. It turns out I have a semi-professional classical saxophonist sitting next to me in Hong Kong. He tells me he stopped performing—couldn't get a job, felt under pressure, lost all joy in it. He shows me a video of himself playing as a teenager. I almost cry—not because of the performance, though it's stellar—but because his gift is now dormant.

There's no comparison between his playing and mine—you might think we were playing entirely different instruments—but it strikes me as so strange: he has this rare, exquisite talent and no longer plays. And here I am—terribly discordant and absolutely desperate to play.

Maybe there are some advantages to taking up an instrument later in life. Less pressure. More freedom.

After my Cody encounter, I rig up a little practice area. The dorm's empty, so I squeak through some blues and Christmas carols. Badly. It's been a while. Thankfully no one—especially Cody (that *would* be embarrassing)—bangs on the door to shut me up.

I hope he starts playing again. It would be criminal not to.

If you're curious, you can find a video of him online—his playing is truly something. But I'll leave it anonymous to respect his privacy.

One day—far in the future—I'll post a YouTube of me playing.

Then again… probably not.

Agnes from Amsterdam

November 28 2018

Hop Inn Mody Hostel, Hong Kong.

Today was mostly spent faffing and researching flights in and out of Vietnam, with several mistimed *"I'm not sure"* conversations back home to Martin. I must learn how to subtract eight hours from my time zone and stop waking people up in the early hours of the morning. Two weeks in a dorm in HK and my brain has gone to mush.

What with:

- the much-anticipated comings and goings of husband Martin and daughter Lucy,
- the *shall we, shan't we go to Vietnam* (and if so, for how long?),
- and the overlaps of my other visitors—who's where, who needs a bed, when?—

I have become as skilled (and as surly) as the polyester-clad Lunn Poly travel clerks I used to rely on back in the '80s. Do you remember the high street, littered with travel agencies? Another retail casualty of the internet age. If they still existed—if there was a Lunn Poly here in Hong Kong—I'd be sat there, instead of juggling three itineraries from a bottom bunk in a poorly lit dorm.

Into my bunk-bed travel agency walks new roomie number 267. I made that up, of course, but it *feels* like over 200 people have come and gone since I arrived.

Agnes from Amsterdam.

Agnes is everything you could want from a roomie. She smiles a lot, is up for adventure, spontaneous, and not at all adverse to sharing a cheap curry in the much-derided Chung King Mansion. She's just stepped off a flight from Vietnam, full of passion for that compelling country and its friendly people. She's buzzing with stories and recommendations and is now wondering whether she might actually want to live there.

Who could resist—Agnes or her new love?

Can you guess who's just booked three weeks in Vietnam?

Yep. The one who was so bereft two weeks ago.

And I might also proudly add that *I* was the one who guided Agnes on her first tour of Tsim Sha Tsui.

What a difference a day—indeed, fourteen days—makes.

Every Picture Tells a Story

November 29 2018
Hop Inn Mody Hostel, Hong Kong.

This could be home

Sometimes, especially as a newbie blogger, inspiration slips through my fingers. I find myself grappling with *blog block*—that dreaded sense of being lost for words. And tonight, I've fallen victim. My thoughts are swirling, and I can't seem to make sense of any of them.

So, with my head firmly on the block, I've decided to let a picture from today do the talking.

It captures a moment when I honestly questioned whether I was still in Hong Kong. The scenery was so breathtaking, it could have been anywhere—Sydney, Ibiza, Croatia, Cornwall, Greece, or Portugal. One of those shimmering, coastal vistas that stops you in your tracks.

I owe special thanks to my new friend Robynne, who showed me a whole different side of the city and coaxed me out to explore Sai Kung. It's moments like these that remind me of the quiet magic found when you dare to step off the beaten track.

When you say *yes*.

When you follow the invitation, even if it's from someone you just met.

Cornwall's Wild Swans

November 30 2018
Lamma Island, Hong Kong.

As December begins — yes, I know, I've jumped the gun on the Christmas songs — I find myself basking in hot sunshine on the serene beaches of Lamma Island. While there may not yet be a partridge in a pear tree, I'm in the company of Cornwall's very own wild swans: three generations of Cornish women, each with her own kind of grace. Baby Tilly, born here on July 19th, 2018; her mama, Aimee; and her po po (maternal grandmother), Liz Rashleigh Mounsey—whom I've written about before. I while away the hours with these three beauties, as they weave me through the island's corners they love most.

Last night, long after dark, I got swept up in another powerful book by Chinese writer and broadcaster Xinran: *What the Chinese Don't Eat*. Someone had left it behind in a café, and lucky me—I picked it up. I'd already read her earlier book, *Message from an Unknown Chinese Mother*, which shares stories of women who gave up or lost their daughters under immense social pressure. It's a searing and unforgettable read.

Xinran is close to me in years, yet light-years ahead in wisdom. Her courage on the page is the kind I aspire to, her words carrying a power that not only inspires but also demands response. Through her work in writing and radio, she has become a powerful voice for Chinese women, exposing the realities of gender inequality and the cultural silence that surrounds it. In 2004, she founded the Mothers' Bridge of Love charity, to help improve the lives of Chinese children everywhere—both those adopted into Western families and those raised in China.

What the Chinese Don't Eat is a collection of short, deeply thoughtful columns originally published in *The Guardian*. One in particular, from September 2003, hit me hard. Titled "Do the foreigners who adopt our girls know how to feed and love them in their arms and hearts?" It speaks directly to the grief, love, and lingering uncertainty that birth mothers live with after adoption.

It was just a few pages long, but it stopped me cold. I won't reproduce it here—you can find it in the book or the *Guardian* archive. Of all the writing on adoption I've come across, this touched me the deepest. It will shake you, comfort you, and leave you changed.

Wild Swans, is the title of Jung Chang's family memoir, which traces the lives of three generations of women—her grandmother, her mother, and herself—through some of China's most turbulent years. Today, with baby Tilly wriggling in the sunshine, I think of lineage. Of what's passed down through the women who raise us, and the ones who couldn't.

As an adoptee, I find myself caught between two sets of stories. The mother who raised me, and the mother who gave birth to me. One was meant to offer structure, security, and survival in a new land. The other—though absent—left behind a silence that I believe shaped me just as much. Sitting here with three generations of Cornish women, and reading Xinran's words the night before, I feel them both more keenly than ever. What gets passed down isn't always visible. But it's there.

I Read the News Today

December 1 2018

Winnie's tireless efforts to get my story into the press have paid off. Today, two major Hong Kong news outlets published online stories about my search for my birth family. I couldn't read either of them—both were in Chinese—but I trusted Winnie when she told me they were beautifully written and sensitively handled.

One article appeared in *Apple Daily*, the other in *HK01*. From what I was told, the stories focused on my journey from England back to Hong Kong, tracing my roots, and the hope of finding my birth mother. They described how I was adopted from Po Leung Kuk orphanage in the 1960s and how, after becoming a grandmother myself, I finally found the courage to return and search for the woman who gave me life.

Update – February 2023

One of the original news stories is no longer accessible, as the outlet has since closed in a changing media landscape. The second article, published by *HK01*, is still live and accessible at the time of writing. You can read it here

https://www.hk01.com/article/264792

I remain deeply grateful to the journalists and photographers who helped share my story with such care and respect.

There are some great photographs—so if you fancy brushing up on your Mandarin (or possibly Cantonese... I wish I could tell!), this one's for you.

Recharge, Reboot

December 2 2018

Hop Inn Mody Hostel, Hong Kong. 23:00

Yesterday, I was depleted. So was my iPhone 5SE, flashing its 2% low battery warning. Apparently, I had a lot of open applications running in the background, quietly draining all my energy.

We are alike and not alike, my mobile and me. The iPhone, with its speedy processor and massive memory, housed in a white rectangle. Me, with my slower but more intricate brain, memory tucked inside 5'1" of human body. Both would suffer if dropped from a great height. Siri could be asked anything, but she couldn't remember the taste of childhood, or the ache of not belonging.

It feels like my own maps/navigation app is always running unless I'm safely ensconced in my hostel. I'm constantly trying to find my way—on foot, by bus, or on the MTR. Always navigating. Always calculating. And while I'm getting better, it's still a constant drain on my energy.

My calculator app runs in the background too. Am I handing over £50 or £5? I'm confident with currency conversions, but when I'm stressed or rushing, I make mistakes. I still remember how angry I was at myself for paying a Greek taxi driver £90 instead of £9. I don't want to repeat that here.

Then there's my security app: always on. Hyper-vigilance. Self-interrogation. Should I carry everything with me and risk losing it? Or lock it all in the wire cage under my bed and trust the 24/7 reception to keep it safe? If I lose my passport now, everything unravels.

Back home, I live by small markers that stitch the week together—yoga, band practice, recycling bins, cleaning flats and watering plants on changeover day. Here, stripped of those stitches, time unravels. I catch myself asking: What day is it? Where am I meant to be? My internal calendar app never closes.

And so, I ask: what might be the human equivalent of closing all the apps and plugging in for a fast charge?

I dump everything into the wire cage and padlock it securely. In go all the devices—phone, modem, charger, cables. Bluetooth keyboard. Headphones. Passport. Driving licence. Cash. Credit cards. Everything of value is stowed beneath my mattress.

I decline an invitation to hike or go on a boat trip. I know for my sanity I must stay alone today,, and close to home. Just me, my swimming costume, a spiral-bound notebook, and my trusty 3B pencil. I head out, following a route I now know by heart, with 5 Hong Kong dollars in my pocket.

I walk to Kowloon Park, unfamiliar in every way, except that it has trees. There are children playing on patches of grass, and birds chirping, seemingly content despite the lack of green and the surplus of concrete. I pause to watch a large wedding party being directed by a photographer. She's keen on capturing unusual antics: the bridegroom piggybacking his new wife; the groomsmen flinging shoes overhead and failing to form a human pyramid; the bride and bridesmaids lifting their dresses and bending over to flash their underwear to bemused guests.

In contrast, on the concrete 'field' opposite, a group of elderly people practise tai chi. They are calm, focused, flowing—everything the wedding party is not. The two scenes capture the extremes you find here in Hong Kong.

I close my eyes to it all. Stretch out on a bench, let the sun warm my face, and fall asleep—unbothered by fears of stolen belongings. It's a short but deep, untroubled nap.

On waking, I try the elderly persons' fitness trail. The signage suggests chin presses, push-ups, hanging from monkey bars. The elderly must be very fit here. I manage the chin presses and push-ups, but halfway across the monkey bars I fall into a small heap. No one sees me, but I make a mental note: don't try that one again.

The sun slips behind the clouds. I head off to do what I do best—ten leisurely lengths at Kowloon's municipal pool.

Recharged, I walk back to the hostel and sleep well—the best night since I arrived.

Martin is always saying we should all turn off the internet for a day. A worldwide digital detox.

He might be onto something.

All Journeys Have Secret Destinations of Which the Traveller Is Unaware

December 3 2018

Hop Inn Mody Hostel, Hong Kong. 8 bed dorm

The title of this post is a quote from German philosopher Martin Buber. I don't think Buber was writing about me accidentally stumbling upon a secret locals' hangout in Hong Kong, but the spirit still fits. He was building on his central "I-Thou" idea—that we find our higher selves when we encounter another person (or nature) without expectation, without trying to extract or define the experience.

I posted a few photos on a Facebook group called *Hong Kong in the '60s*, not expecting any response. I was wrong. So many wonderful people responded—hundreds of them. They shared the post, sent kind wishes. I met up with some, and kept talking with others. It's moments like these that make this whole trip feel worthwhile. Even if I never find my birth family, *something* has shifted. *I* have been changed, for the better.

A 70-year-old man posted in the same group, asking about coming back to Hong Kong. Could he do it on a budget? When would be the best time? Would he even make it? Should he try?

I'm not yet 70, but I know what I'd say to him: Yes. Try.

One day, when I have more time, I'd love to write something called *Hong Kong on a Shoestring for the Over-50s*. HK is always listed among the most expensive cities in the world—but it *is* possible to visit on a budget, if you know how. And now, I do.

But would this man believe me?

After all, a friend recently tagged me in a Facebook post where I'm standing in front of a Bentley. In another photo, I'm gazing out over a marina full of millionaires' boats. Understandably, he might be confused. He wouldn't know that all this wasn't mine, but generously offered by another group member I'd met online. He wouldn't picture me starting that same day in the dark, scrabbling around in a cage under a bunk bed, trying to find something clean to wear. Or that I'd begun the day expecting a hike, not an unexpected brush with luxury.

Today I met up with Winnie and had another "living like a local" experience—she brought me to her weekly massage. Ninety minutes of being pummelled back into shape. But this wasn't a UK-style massage: no scented candles, no floating petals, no ambient music or Buddha statues. Just a curtained cubicle, a plastic chair for my clothes, and a masseur in a pink nylon overall that reminded me of school dinner ladies.

She didn't introduce herself or ask any of the usual health questions. Perhaps because I didn't speak Cantonese, she just got on with it. Her pace and pressure never changed. At one point, Winnie (in the next cubicle) asked if I was okay—maybe she heard my muffled whimpering. Not wanting to sound ungrateful, I mumbled "Yes." I lied. It was the most brutal massage I've ever had. Not for the faint-hearted or the fragile-bodied. I was relieved when the masseur gave my paper-pantied bottom a brisk slap and said, in perfect English, "All finish. You dress now."

Over dim sum lunch, I tried to sound appreciative of my bruising. I had to resist showing Winnie the fresh badges of honour colouring my skin. She had treated me, and spoken so fondly of this ritual of hers—as if it were relaxing. Winnie is made of sterner stuff than me. This is what she does to unwind? I make a mental note to buy her a good book.

But I should know by now: taking it easy isn't part of Winnie's psyche. As soon as lunch ends, we're off again—posting her Christmas cards and meeting a 70-year-old woman who was never adopted, raised instead in Fanling Orphanage. She lived her entire childhood in care, and even remained there into adulthood. That saddened me. But I've since been told that many of the older orphans formed strong chosen families and looked back fondly on their years in care.

Still, a comment shared by one of them stayed with me. She once said, perhaps as a joke, that she hadn't been adopted or sent abroad because she "wasn't pretty enough." It was a bitter thing to hear. I hope it wasn't true—but even as a joke, it reveals how easily beauty standards creep into our sense of worth, even as children.

To that 70-year-old man who posted in the group asking if he should come to Hong Kong, I'd say this:

Yes, you should. And yes, you can.

Do it. Just do it.

Come here—right now, if you can.

But maybe… give the local massage a miss.

An Unexpected Invitation

December 4 2018

Hong Kong Social Welfare Department, North Point

After my previous attempt in 2002, when I first wrote to the HKSWD requesting access to my adoption records—and was told they couldn't help—here I am, bewildered by an unexpected invitation.

Urged on by Winnie, I'd written to them again just days after arriving in Hong Kong. She was keen to see their copy of my birth certificate and my mother's statement. My copy of that statement is so faint, and she wanted to read the Chinese characters of my birth father's name properly.

To my surprise, I received an email in response.

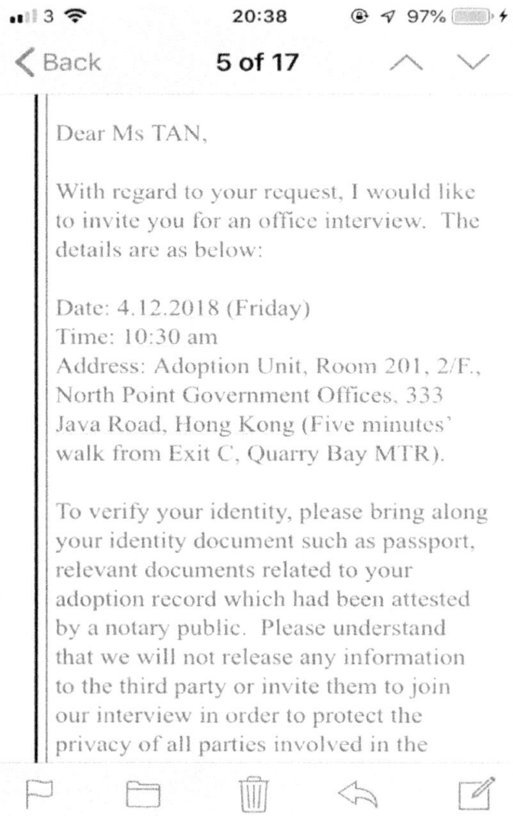
3 20:38 97%
Back 5 of 17

Dear Ms TAN,

With regard to your request, I would like to invite you for an office interview. The details are as below:

Date: 4.12.2018 (Friday)
Time: 10:30 am
Address: Adoption Unit, Room 201, 2/F., North Point Government Offices, 333 Java Road, Hong Kong (Five minutes' walk from Exit C, Quarry Bay MTR).

To verify your identity, please bring along your identity document such as passport, relevant documents related to your adoption record which had been attested by a notary public. Please understand that we will not release any information to the third party or invite them to join our interview in order to protect the privacy of all parties involved in the

I had to go.

There was a catch, though: I wasn't allowed to bring Winnie with me. Government offices here have strict rules about who can accompany individuals. Apparently, you can take, no one.

Winnie, ever protective, warned me about the possible demeanour of Chinese officials—some, she said, could be brutal and officious.

Feeling a mix of nerves and uncertainty—quite unlike me—I retreated to the comforting banality of a Starbucks. Coffee. Cake. Familiar shapes and smells. Not the most sophisticated form of emotional refuge, but exactly what I needed.

Wish me luck, it feels like I'm stepping into something unknown.

Room 201. The Other Brother

December 5 2018

Hop Inn Mody Hostel, Hong Kong. 8 bed dorm

The meeting is over now.

I'm still not sure how to talk about it.

I walked in alone and left feeling like I'd come apart.

What follows is what I wrote once I could breathe again.

This is the blog I wrote after my unexpected meeting with social worker Celia (I've changed her name so as not to get her into trouble) at the HKSWD. It was during this meeting I first learned they held a detailed case file opened in 1961. When I wrote in 2002, they never mentioned it. Now I understand they were likely bound by Chinese Privacy Law, which protects the identities of those named within the file.

As I reinstate this blog, I'm sitting in the quiet reception at Hop Inn Mody, on a big Apple Mac with a proper keyboard—a luxury after days typing on my phone. It's 3pm. Saxophone jazz plays softly. I'm trying to ground myself.

This morning was about regrouping. A long sleep. Porridge with ginger and honey. Green tea. A hot shower. Washing my clothes. Tidying the area around my bunk. Rehanging the curtain for privacy. Meditation. Simple tasks that helped me restore order. I smiled through them, willing myself back to hope.

Because yesterday, I was undone. Room 201, Adoption Services. A small, stark space. Just a table, two chairs, and faded posters—adoption ads and a complaints contact. I arrived early but still managed to get lost, flustered, panicking. I had five minutes to spare. Just enough time to read the only English book in the waiting area: *Spot Goes to the Farm.* A pull the tab book. Strange comfort. I'd read that same book to my son Tom three decades ago, so many times that all the tabs fell off.

In that room, I began to lose perspective. I realised how distorted my sense of self had become. Being away from home amplifies everything. I felt like a child—raw, vulnerable, and overwhelmed. The search for family, for identity, suddenly felt too big. I wanted comfort, I wanted a mum.

At 10:30am, I met Celia. She gave me two and a half hours. Warm but constrained by law. She had my decade-long correspondence in front of her. I asked for a better copy of my mother's Statutory Declaration, hoping for the Chinese characters of my father's name. At first, she was hesitant. But as I shared what I'd already learned from Warwickshire County Council, her tone shifted. She realised I wasn't starting from scratch. That recognition felt like oxygen.

Wanting to lighten the mood, I asked about her daughter. She showed me a photo—eight years old, bright smile. It reminded us both we were more than this room.

Celia explained root tracing wasn't her main job. Her role was adoptions. Privacy law was strict. But as we spoke, a professional connection formed. I shared my background in counselling. We spoke about attachment theory, the emotional complexity for adoptees. She understood.

Then she left to photocopy my passport. Took longer than expected. I joked to myself she'd gone to Starbucks. But when she returned, she carried a different file. Older. Thicker. On loan from the archives. She reminded me she couldn't show me everything. But this file—overflowing with details—was *mine*. And not mine. I couldn't touch it, photograph it, or read it fully. But I caught glimpses.

She spoke of a Village Chief, Mr. Yau, who helped my mother. Gave her rice when she was surviving on relief food. Accompanied her to the Government Office in Yuen Long. I felt a strange mix of gratitude and rage. How could this have been hidden for so long?

I craned my neck to read the upside-down text. I saw the names of my siblings. My birth father's name. I wasn't allowed to know them. But I learned that none of them were adopted. Celia told me my mother was known as the mother of "Wood and Water Boy."

She wrote out Wong Tin in Chinese for Winnie. Said my mother was likely 40 when she had me. And that landed like a punch. If she was 40, she wouldn't still be alive. I'd always held on to the faint hope she might be. But now I knew—I was too late. And yet, I began to speak to her in my mind: "I know more now, mum. I'm coming closer."

Then came more: I was her *seventh* child, not fourth. Two died in infancy. My mother was illiterate. She lived in Melon Garden—in a broken hut. Rent-free, thanks to a friend's employer. She was from Shuntak, now part of Foshan. Foshan. The same place I stayed when I visited China. I'd gone there by chance, invited by a girl I met in St Ives. Her father had taught me to make dumplings. To brew Oolong tea. All this, before I knew my mother had come from there.

This is more than a search. It's a return. A reconnection. A remembering.

Celia kept reading. A letter from Mrs. Gregory, a UK social worker, describing my adoptive parents' house in Leamington Spa as a "ramshackle little house that somehow manages to be okay." Notes about my adoptive father's time in Hong Kong. My adoptive mother's belief she could do better than her own adoptive mother. That irony hit hard.

Fragments. Anecdotes. Bits of my life I'd never known. That I now had to absorb in a single sitting, without notes, without pause.

Celia told me I'd stayed with a foster family after leaving Po Leung Kuk. A Caucasian family named Starkey. A transitional home before England. I remembered the blow-up Father Christmas, stamped with 'Made in Hong Kong'. The toy was just like me, my family used to joke, as I had a dark blue Mongolian birthmark, like a stamp, on my bottom. Unfamiliar to English doctors. My mother even wrote to ask what it was.

That mark became my unofficial origin story. I remember hiding under the pantry shelf in my new home, where my BOAC bag had gone mouldy, clutching that inflatable Father Christmas. He had a hole in his head I'd tried to fix with sellotape. When I realised he couldn't be blown up again, I felt it in my body—both of us crumpled and deflated.

Celia continued. A report from when I was ten weeks old. Sticky eyes. Anaemic skin. Then, at nine months: chubby, sweet, jolly. It hurt to hear. And yet it made me smile.

She said my Chinese zodiac sign was the Rat. Clever, resourceful, a survivor. In the legend, the Rat won the race across the river by hitching a ride on the Ox's back, then leaping ahead at the last second to claim victory. That cunning and opportunistic nature helped the Rat succeed—but only with the Ox's strength. Right now, I didn't feel clever or strategic. I needed an Ox—someone steady and strong to carry me the rest of the way.

Then casually, almost as an afterthought, she said: "You had another older brother who was sold to a Village Chief."

I stared at her. Another brother? Sold? The words didn't make sense. I couldn't take any more in. It was too much. I felt myself pulling away—not physically, but somewhere inside, everything started to shut down.

I ended the meeting. Thanked her, too quickly. I fled the building, heart racing, mouth dry, reeling.

I found an expensive restaurant full of office workers. Ignored the elaborate menu. Ordered plain boiled rice and a Blue Girl beer. My comfort food.

I wanted to howl. Instead, I curled up in my hostel bunk, curtains drawn, trying not to cry. Trying to stay quiet.

Later, I wrote this:

"Dear Yuk Lan, Next time, maybe bring someone who loves you—even if they wait outside. Don't go to Mandarin class the same night.

Especially not one full of native speakers. Don't rely solely on Google Maps. Trust yourself. Sometimes, you already know the way home."

Blue Girl, Sad Girl

December 6 2018

Hop Inn Mody Hostel, Hong Kong. 8 bed dorm

Today, I gave myself the day off from writing.

The pictures I took say more than words could. There's a selfie—my face says it all.

A beer—Blue Girl. It matched my mood.

And my meditation app gently reminding me: *you can't get rid of these feelings, but you can shift your perspective.*

It wasn't much. But it helped.

Family Matters

December 7 2018

Hop Inn Mody Hostel, Hong Kong. 8 bed dorm

The meeting's over now, but I'm still turning it over in my mind. Celia's follow up email anchors the details—reassures me I did, in fact, hear what I thought I heard. That I'm turning over the right pieces.

The email reads :

Dear Laura

It's great to meet you on 4th December 2018.

I checked our old record again and found that the information in our file is consistent with the information collected by you in the UK and HK.

I would like to supplement the information of your birth family (at the time of relinquishment in 1961) as follows :

Birth mother, aged 40, illiterate, married with first husband at the age of 18 in Hong Kong, native of Shun Tak, living on relief food and a certain amount of rice from the village chief.

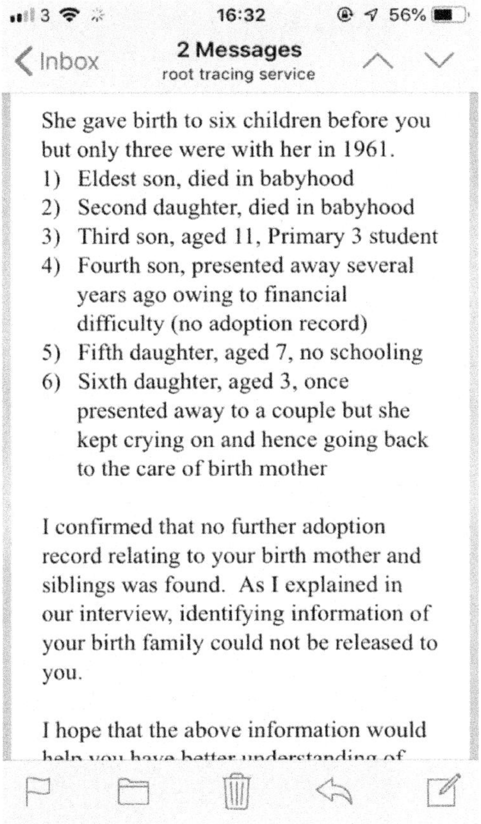
3 16:32 56%

Inbox **2 Messages** root tracing service

She gave birth to six children before you but only three were with her in 1961.

1) Eldest son, died in babyhood
2) Second daughter, died in babyhood
3) Third son, aged 11, Primary 3 student
4) Fourth son, presented away several years ago owing to financial difficulty (no adoption record)
5) Fifth daughter, aged 7, no schooling
6) Sixth daughter, aged 3, once presented away to a couple but she kept crying on and hence going back to the care of birth mother

I confirmed that no further adoption record relating to your birth mother and siblings was found. As I explained in our interview, identifying information of your birth family could not be released to you.

I hope that the above information would help you have better understanding of

Celia was kind. I believe she genuinely wanted to help me. But she also seemed worried—worried that if she said too much, her job could be at risk. I don't want to jeopardise her in any way.

Now, as I edit these blogs with the hope of publishing my memoir, I find myself already thinking about how to tell the truth while protecting the people in it. Hopefully someone with more experience of memoir writing will help guide me through that delicate balance. It feels like a good problem to have—because it means the memoir might actually make it out into the world. I'll cross that bridge when I need to.

And as I revisit that experience with Celia, I remember again how I wasn't allowed to touch the file. Not even photograph it. Everything I learned had to be taken in on the spot—upside down across a desk, while

Celia read fragments aloud. I hadn't expected a file. Let alone one this big. Let alone what was inside it.

It was bewildering. Overwhelming. And, yes—enraging.

All of it—just sitting in a cabinet. Hong Kong Social Welfare had it all along. My adoptive parents never helped me look. No one thought I might need to know who I am.

The shock of it didn't wear off for days. And the anger—it still flickers. Even now, as I write this, I feel it rising. The betrayal. The grief for what was withheld.

I'm also mindful of other adoptees trying to trace their roots through the HKSWD. I don't want my story—or the telling of it—to close doors for them. The more time I spend reflecting, the more I realise I'm just one of millions. Root tracing is far bigger than I imagined.

And it's not just Hong Kong. There are those who grew up in orphanages here and were never adopted, only ageing out of care in young adulthood. Others were informally adopted by Chinese families, with no records at all. Then there are transracial adoptees like me—sent abroad as part of the United Nations Refugee Programme in the 1960s. So many of us. All orphans. But each story is different.

And that's just Hong Kong.

If I begin to think about adoptees from Vietnam, Cambodia, China, India—and then beyond Asia—I start to feel insignificant. Absurd. A single thread in a vast and tangled weave.

All day, I've been turning over thoughts about families. My birth family—larger than I'd ever imagined.

The idea that I have *another* big brother—given away and lost to time—leaves me dumbfounded. It's one of those rare moments where a cliché feels absolutely right:

You could have knocked me down with a feather.

Wondering about him, my other birth siblings. My adoptive family.

And the little family I've left back home in the UK.

Family matters. Yes, they do.
Family matters.

Bright Lights, Big City

December 8 2018

Hop Inn Mody Hostel, Hong Kong. 8 bed dorm

You'd think that being in the most illuminated city on the planet, I'd be lucid, lit up, overflowing with lightbulb moments. But I'm not.

Today I pounded the streets, wandering through designer shops, hoping for inspiration. The windows are exquisite—little masterpieces of display. Who knew there were so many ways to fashion a reindeer? Sleek antlers, twinkling noses, red velvet bows.

I'm not drawn to how the wealthier Hong Kong women dress—too polished, too perfectionist—but some glide past like they've stepped straight out of Vogue. Impeccably turned out, clad in clothes to die for.

I feel shabby beside them. Out of place.

So I give in to temptation. Retail therapy, Hong Kong style. I lose myself in the joy of trying things on—maxi dresses in red and gold, stripey trouser suits, Nordic Fair Isle jumpers. The magic is in the fit—everything just right, unlike back home where sleeves and hems always seem made for taller lives.

At the till, a manageable total flashes up. *Ker-ching.* I hand over my card and feel a strange elation—ease, lightness. Consumerism is so seductive here. It would be dangerously easy to get addicted.

For a moment, I belong. I'm running with the tribe. And yes, in this city of endless consumption, shopping really *is* a hobby.

Back at the dorm, I unpack the bags and stare blankly at what I've bought. Gorgeous things—but useless for my life in Cornwall. Useless for dusty roads in Vietnam.

Don't panic, Martin. It was only H&M, not Chanel or Hermès. Everything can go back tomorrow—30-day returns.

Still, it was fun while it lasted. A temporary high. A break from all the searching.

But I think I'll cherish the memory of wandering Hong Kong—its streets, its lights, its unexpected moments—more than anything I could ever carry home in a bag.

What Is Black, White and Red All Over?

December 9 2018 18:48

Hop Inn Mody Hostel, Hong Kong. 8 bed dorm

As I type, the aroma of warm roasted chestnuts fills the air. I'm wrapped in the Icelandic-style wool jumper over the flowing red dress I decided to keep from yesterday's H&M spree. The temperature has dipped; it's beginning to feel a lot like Christmas.

This morning, the dorm was empty when I emerged around 9:30. Most of my roommates, here for just a few days, rise early to maximize their time. I'm making every moment count too, albeit in my own way.

My friend Yo commented on my blog, asking to see some of the H&M items before I return them. Seizing the opportunity, I transformed the vacant dorm into my personal runway. Black, white, and red have always been staples in my wardrobe, a theme echoed in H&M's Christmas collection. I shared photos from my first visit to Hong Kong in the '80s, showcasing the clothes I bought then. Predictable, perhaps, but even then I embraced my black, white, and red fashion groove.

I strive to be a considerate roommate. Past experiences have taught me the value of this—like the time a fellow traveller took a 3 a.m. half-hour shower, or another whose nocturnal noises resembled a distressed frog. Then there was the early riser who, at 4 a.m., repacked her rucksack using noisy crinkly plastic bags. Drawing from these lessons, I quietly organised my belongings and headed to the pool.

Near the hostel, the chic K11 shopping arcade boasts a covered stage for Christmas performances. Today, a children's singing school, aptly named Red Vocal, entertained shoppers with carols. The young performers, with their shiny black hair, donned red, black, and white outfits—sequined red Santa hats with white pom-poms, girls in red dresses with black sashes, boys in black lederhosen with red shirts.

Watching them, a realisation struck: my affinity for this colour palette likely traces back to my earliest memories. Given that my first gift was a blow-up Father Christmas (red suit, white beard, black belt) that accompanied me to England, it's no wonder these colours resonate so deeply.

Today offered other insights that, while seemingly minor, hold significance for me. I'd naively assumed cancer wasn't a major issue in Hong Kong, given the general healthiness of its people. Obesity is rare; many engage in self-care practices like tai chi and stretching. Yet, attending the "Hong Kong Cancer Day" event at Kowloon Park revealed the stark reality. Cancer is a prevalent concern here, as it is globally.

The event featured local amateur groups performing on a makeshift stage. I felt a pang of longing, imagining myself playing a set with the Hong Kong equivalent of the St Ives Concert Band. The performers, though not all polished, radiated joy and festive spirit. Singers, musicians, dancers of all ages showcased their talents, with traditional Chinese musicians displaying notable skill. Martial arts demonstrations evoked nostalgia for my tae kwon do days.

Wandering the surrounding stalls, I engaged with volunteers eager to share their causes, despite language barriers. Many activities catered to children, allowing me to indulge my inner child. At one booth, I attempted to craft a felt Father Christmas decoration. Applying glue to the wrong side of the pre-cut beard, I struggled until a teenage volunteer, switching effortlessly to English, offered help. "Don't worry, you won't see the glue when it dries," she reassured me. The embarrassment of needing help with a child's craft, compounded by my lack of Cantonese, was humbling.

I left the decoration unfinished, yielding my seat to a patiently waiting little girl. Continuing my exploration, I collected vegan literature—useful for when Lucy arrives next month. I've learned that some vegetarian dishes here contain hidden meats or fish sauces, so vigilance is essential.

Many have asked about the next steps in my root-tracing journey. One leaflet from the event introduced a women's charity in my mother's former neighbourhood. I plan to contact them, hoping someone might recall my mother or sisters. The "Hong Kong in the 1960s" Facebook group continues to be a wellspring of support. Winnie, ever persistent, offers ideas and gentle reminders for tasks I've yet to complete. The generosity and warmth I've encountered, both online and in person, are overwhelming. Despite my linguistic shortcomings, strangers extend their hands in friendship.

Martin arrives on Wednesday. I'm eager to share a small studio flat in Sai Kung with him, to cook properly again, and to experience being part of a couple here. The studio overlooks Sai Kung harbour—an exquisitely designed space with an echo of our own flat back home. I'm counting down to Christmas and our trip to Vietnam. A respite from root-tracing is just what I need.

While I won't miss the 8-bed dorm, certain staff members have left an impression, especially Rosa, who cleans on weekends. Originally from the Philippines, Rosa is always chatty, inquiring about my well-being. Today, I turned the question to her. She revealed she has two grandchildren in the Philippines—a boy and a girl, one in college, the other recently graduated. "They are my children now," she said softly. Her son passed away this year from a heart attack at 40. After his wife's death from a brain aneurysm in 2014, he was struggling. After her last visit to the Philippines, Rosa had just bought tickets for him and the children to visit her in Hong Kong when tragedy struck. She had been home for only two days when he died. I hugged her, words failing me. Rosa whispered, "Thank you for hearing my story," as she wiped away a tear—not hers, but mine.

Reflecting on my recent post, "Family Matters," I'm reminded of the importance of telling our loved ones just how much they mean to us. I know I'm going to.

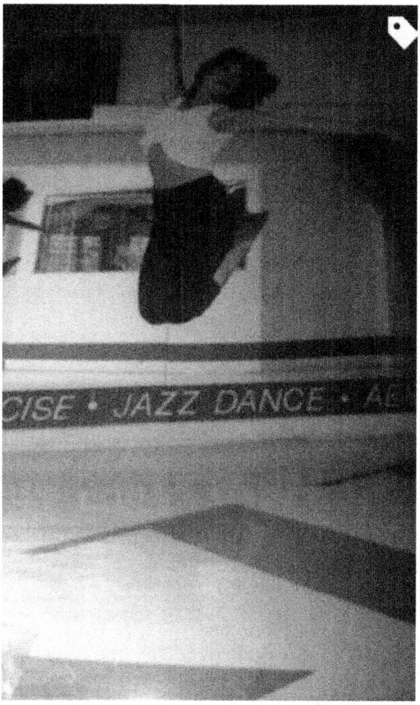

Even when I visited Hong Kong in the 80s, I embraced black, white and red

Not Just Another New Kid in Town

December 10 2018

Hop Inn Mody Hostel, Hong Kong. 8 bed dorm

About a year ago, a woman reached out to me via Facebook, inquiring about starting a lunch club for the lonely and elderly in St Ives. She believed I'd be a good resource, noting my local insights and community involvement. To be recognized as a "local" in Cornwall—a place known for its cautious embrace of newcomers—was a badge of honour. Martin might have joked about widening the doorways to accommodate my swelling pride.

This morning, I struck up a conversation with Lauren, a tall, cheerful backpacker making her way back to New Zealand after a month teaching English in mainland China. She was grappling with Hong Kong's steep prices, especially after having her accommodation and basic meals covered during her teaching stint. In contrast, just yesterday, I met a Belgian woman working in Korea, eagerly stockpiling chocolate here due to import restrictions back home.

Lauren and I shared a modest breakfast of porridge oats with ginger and honey while brainstorming budget-friendly activities. I suggested the classic Star Ferry ride to Hong Kong Island, followed by a ferry to Lamma Island. I provided her with a map, pointed out the piers, and recommended returning after dark to witness the Tsim Sha Tsui skyline illuminated from the water. Additionally, I mentioned affordable vegetarian options in Chungking Mansions, cautioning her about the occasional inclusion of hidden meats.

While Lauren embarked on her adventure, I spent the day deepening my own roots. Wandering through familiar streets, I exchanged greetings with locals who now recognise me. At Kowloon Park's training pool—typically reserved for the elderly and those seeking a quieter swim— I joined gentle exercises with elderly women. In the pool beside us, a lane for swimmers with failing sight—a glimpse of something I might one day need because of my severe myopia, and it steadied me. By 4 p.m., the pool welcomed groups of schoolchildren for lessons, a lively contrast to the morning's tranquillity.

Feeling content from my day's routine, I returned home to read, write, and prepare for my upcoming move to Sai Kung. I'm reserving the more tourist-centric activities for when Martin and Lucy arrive, saving my energy for their visit.

As I brewed tea, Lauren returned, beaming from her day out. She clutched a takeout curry from Chungking Mansions and returned my map. "I had the best day," she said. "Your recommendations were spot on—better than if I'd asked a local."

Twenty-seven nights in Hong Kong, and I'm offering insights that rival those of residents? I smiled, accepting her compliment with a silent cheer. This city moves at a relentless pace, but I'm finding my rhythm. Hong Kong, I'm ready for you.

Sai Kung Can Wait

December 11 2018

Hop Inn Mody Hostel, Hong Kong. 8 bed dorm

I've rented a tiny apartment in Sai Kung to show Martin another side of my birthplace. His visits for business left him thinking Hong Kong was only grey and drizzly. I want him to see the lush green Hong Kong I've come to know.

Eighty percent of Hong Kong is apparently made up of country parks. There are hidden beaches, coves, mountains, and hiking trails. I've seen views here that rival Cornwall. Sai Kung will be the perfect base for his introduction to this brighter, wilder version of the city.

Toni, the Cathay Pacific pilot renting me the studio, messaged to say it's ready earlier than expected. I thank her and say I'll be over soon.

I could have rushed there hours ago—but did I?

No. It's 2:05 p.m., and I'm still here at Hop Inn Mody, blogging. I find it hard to tear myself away.

I make a final lunch of rice, spinach, and sweet potato, and strike up a conversation with the newest roommate, Ciara, from Northern Ireland. A teacher and a free spirit, she's about to move to Australia and is travelling while she waits for her visa. She's climbed parts of Everest, spent a month in China, and now she's heading to Vietnam.

She embodies the spirit of the hostel—adventurous, open, alive.

I thrive on stories like hers. They remind me that many still reach across borders, learning from one another, sharing lives and spaces. That feels far more hopeful than walls or the cry of 'not in my backyard.' I know it's a sensitive subject—one that has split families and divided friends. But isn't it worth revisiting? Worth holding space for? Still, now probably isn't the moment to dive into geopolitics. I should be packing.

I realise I'm completely out of touch with UK news. What's happening with Brexit? Are we still planning to leave in March? Maybe I'm better off staying here. After all, back home the chorus seems to be: go back where you came from.

I shake off the thought and turn to something I can control: my phone. My old iPhone SE takes terrible photos, which is a shame because I want to capture this place—the strange, beautiful energy of Hop Inn. It isn't just budget accommodation. It feels like an eccentric home, full of quiet details and shared moments.

Before I arrived, I'd been trying to cut down on phone use. The screen time reports were brutal. And yet I caught myself yearning for a phone with a better camera—maybe the Huawei P20 Pro with its three Leica lenses. I resisted. If I'd bought it, I'd probably be even more glued to the screen. And I'd also be broke.

Everyone here seems permanently attached to their phones—walking, riding the MTR, even eating without looking up. I don't admire the behaviour, but I'm not sure I'd be any better with a flashy upgrade.

Yesterday I was in McDonald's. People sat in rows of booths separated by strips of fake green grass, eating from plastic containers with plastic utensils, eyes fixed on their screens. Some booths even had upside-down turf hanging from the ceiling—luxury, perhaps. The diners were mostly office workers dressed in blacks, greys, navies, fawns.

I thought of Ciara—her vibrant Nepalese silk trousers, alive with pink, blue, yellow, and purple—and I felt a twinge of sadness. Sad for the McDonald's diners. Sad for this strange world we've created.

Not long ago, I was close enough to touch the huts where refugees still live—shelters like the ones my mother sought when she escaped mainland China.

It's a poignant reminder of the worlds we've constructed and the potential paradises we've paved over. How does that Joni Mitchell song go?

"Don't It always seem to go, you don't know what you've got 'til it's gone?...They've paved paradise and put up a parking lot."

Everlasting Birthday

December 12 2018
Sai Kung, Hong Kong

How lucky Martin is to have a two-day, two-country birthday.

I awoke today in Sai Kung to sunlight and a view of mountains, boats, trees, and sea. And a whole king-sized bed to myself. No roomies. No wondering if it was too early to jump up and risk waking someone. I didn't have to get dressed under the covers in a cramped bunk before stepping out into darkness.

What a great start.

I cooked on a hob for the first time in a month—scrambled eggs on toast. What luxury. The perfect beginning to a day that could only get better with a 2:30 p.m. rendezvous at Hong Kong airport to greet Martin, flying in from the UK.

Martin (aka Mr. P and Wookiee) began his birthday—December 11—in Stratford-upon-Avon with Tom, Lisa, and baby Phoebe. But once he boarded the plane to Hong Kong, he immediately lost eight hours of his special day.

We made up for it here. We opened our Christmas cards together, and he unwrapped his birthday cards and presents. There were some fabulous ones, but for me, the very best was a card made from a photograph of baby Phoebe wearing a plum pudding hat. She looked utterly adorable.

I may never find my mother.

But I am reminded that part of her lives on through Phoebe.

From Dai Pai Dong to High Society. My Love Affair with Street Food

December 14 2018
Stanley

It's funny what holds—what persists across distance, adoption, and time. For me, it's not language or customs or holidays. It's street food. Somehow, the girl raised on fish fingers in England still finds her way back to her Chinese roots through a plastic bowl of wonton noodles, steaming in an alleyway stall. Yes, you can take this girl out of the Dai Pai Dong, but you can't take the Dai Pai Dong out of the girl.

You've probably heard the saying, "You can take the girl out of the trailer park, but you can't take the trailer park out of the girl." Usually, it's meant as a jab—a way to suggest that no matter how far someone travels, they'll always carry their rough edges.

But for me, it's not about class—it's about connection.

Dai pai dongs are open-air food stalls in Hong Kong, the kind that would be shut down instantly by UK health inspectors. But I *love* them. The food, the smells, the experience: simple, no-nonsense soul food—steaming soup, stir-fried veg, noodles, sizzling meat. I love sitting on wobbly stools, crammed around tin tables with strangers. If you're lucky, there's a paper tablecloth held down by sticky, unlabelled bottles of soy and chilli sauce. Heaven.

"What have you been eating for the last month?" Martin asks, genuinely puzzled.

I grin and lead him down a narrow alley near our Sai Kung apartment, where the air is thick with sizzling spice and smoke. He doesn't get it—he sees a hygiene risk. I see home.

Even back in England, I've always chosen the street option: a baked potato from a market stall over McDonald's any day. Beans and cheese. Cottage cheese and garlic butter. In Israel, it was falafel. In Turkey, roasted corn. Sardines grilled on oil drums in Portugal. Chestnuts at Christmas markets. Pop-up feasts in Marrakech. Anywhere there's food that comes with heat, chaos, and history—I'm there.

Sure, I enjoy the high life too—but anyone who knows me knows I get just as much joy (maybe more) from skip-diving and charity shops, from unearthing a vintage cashmere scarf or rescuing hotel lobby Christmas trees to raise money for the orphanage I was once in. I see beauty where others wouldn't look.

When I first moved to Cornwall, I lived in a flat above the harbour in St Ives, filled with junk-shop treasures and reclaimed wood. In Stratford-upon-Avon, I knew exactly which night the shops threw out cardboard—perfect for art projects. I've always been a finder. A forager. A seeker of meaning in the overlooked.

Yesterday, I convinced Martin to eat at a dai pai dong in Stanley. My kind of hidden gem. I slurped thick wonton noodles with locals and a few in-the-know tourists, practising my rusty Putonghua with two giggling teenagers from mainland China. And somewhere in the swirl of steam and laughter, a memory surfaced—of Friday nights with my boyfriend's family back in the UK, eating sweet and sour pork and prawn crackers. "Fake" Chinese food, but still… a beginning.

Later that evening, we were invited to dine at the Royal Hong Kong Yacht Club—one of the city's oldest and most exclusive establishments. White linen. Vellum menus. Polished glassware. It was beautiful. But when I think about those two meals—one carried to me on white linen, the other slurped from a plastic bowl on a folding stool—only one fed my soul. Luxury has its moments. But give me a bowl of noodles on a bustling street corner, and I'm home.

Let's Go Fly a Kite

December 15 2018
Tap Mun Island

Sometimes I found myself chasing moments—not answers—just moments that might carry memory, magic, or the kind of joy I imagined my mother once knew. I didn't always say that out loud. I just said, "Let's go fly a kite."

"Let's fly a kite," I said to Martin. "Or maybe we could camp and pretend we're back in Cornwall. Burn our faces in hot sunshine and eat the finest seafood. Let's drink beer, bump into the odd cow or two and visit a 400-year-old temple or find the pirate tunnel."

He looked at me like I might've gone mad. But it was all possible—I knew it from the guidebooks stacked in our apartment. Martin was willing, and we had managed to tick off a few items on my Sai Kung to-do list.

And then, Tap Mun, or Grass Island. It felt like we'd stepped onto the Cornish coastal path in the height of summer—with a few beautiful exceptions: the temples where incense burned all day long, the Hakka women in traditional dress, squatting and chattering as they worked.

Watching them, I thought about my mother. I wondered if, before life broke open under the weight of loss and poverty, she ever came here. Maybe before her husband died, before she had to give me up. Maybe she once ferried across the water to this island, and for a day—just one—she breathed easy. Maybe she felt the same wonder and joy I felt on Grass Island today. I hope so.

Two Line Blogging. The Challenges of Being a Couple

December 16 2018

Sai Kung

Some days, the emotional weight of the search was too much. Other days, the greatest challenge was simply being in a room together.

Setting: an open-plan studio apartment in Sai Kung. No balcony. No separate rooms. No escape routes.

Martin: *"I need to go to sleep now."*

Me: *"I need to write my blog now..."*

Sometimes, that's all you need to sum up the shape of a relationship—two truths, side by side, quietly colliding.

Inebriated Blog Musings

December 17 2018
Sai Kung

Blogging publicly is becoming harder, I realise. The words don't flow as easily as they did at the start. It feels disjointed now. The more people involved in the day I want to write about, the more fragmented and uneven it becomes.

Should I write about the people I've spent the day with? Should I ask their permission first? What's the etiquette when it comes to blogging about others?

When I was only blogging about myself, it was much simpler.

Well, that's just my humble opinion. But I've only been doing this for about thirty days—and I've had a bit too much wine and gin to be let loose on a blog right now.

In general, I still believe a blog worth its salt should be genuine and transparent. Once you start editing and second-guessing, it loses the spark that makes it worth reading. Then again, maybe that's just the gin talking.

When I started this blog, I was flying solo—soaring, loop-the-looping, sometimes crashing and burning. Now I'm coupled up again and spending more time with friends, and things have changed.

Don't get me wrong—it's lovely to share this with others. But it's shifting the way I blog. I have less time, and fewer insights. I meditate less. I eat and drink more, which dulls my brain and slows down my powers of observation. I accumulate more things than are good for me—especially considering I'm flying to Vietnam tomorrow with only one piece of hand luggage.

Luckily, all these worries are forgotten tonight as we head out for a final dinner in Sai Kung. The restaurant we've chosen is called Padstow.

"Padstow?! Blimey, she's really lost it," I can almost hear you say.

But no—it's true. And I have a blurry photo of me wearing my Made in Hong Kong t-shirt, holding a Padstow menu, to prove it.

Missing Pieces

On December 11th, Martin flew over from England to join me in Hong Kong. We had both hoped that, by the time he arrived, I might have found my birth family—or at least uncovered some promising leads.

No such luck.

We had booked flights to Vietnam as a kind of Plan B, and in the end, we spent nearly four weeks there together.

I haven't included all my blog entries from that time. They might just belong in the *next* book.

But I've included one entry from that trip—New Year's Eve, 2019.

My final Vietnam blog.

It feels pertinent to this memoir.

These Are a Few of My Favourite Things

December 31 2018
Vietnam

The last day of 2018. It started well, and I'm grateful for so many things. I thought I'd celebrate the end of the year by listing a few:

1. The ability—and time—to travel to other countries, physically, financially, and a reasonable brain to plan it all.
2. The chance to spend time in Hong Kong to search for my birth family—and all the help, love, and support I've received, especially from Winnie and www.look4mama.com
3. English is widely spoken, and I can mostly be understood.
4. Really good health. Especially grateful for my thawed-out frozen shoulder, which caused me so much pain for over a year and has now fully healed. I'm thankful my body knows how to mend itself.
5. Family—like Martin and Lucy—who are accompanying me in person for part of this quest.
6. Friends and family back home who are travelling with me virtually, thanks to........
7. Technology: Wi-Fi, mobile phones, portable keyboard, headphones.
8. Daily meditation.
9. Almost daily swimming—today in a pool just seconds from a cheap but luxurious Vietnamese hotel suite.
10. A long, piping-hot bath after a rather cold swim.
11. Food of every kind—from Europe and Asia, hot and cold, sweet and savoury. The chance to sample, savour, and, in some cases, reject without being too wasteful.
12. My Christmas karaoke microphone and speaker.

13. Streamed music of my choice, including corny Christmas songs and Dire Straits' Brothers in Arms.
14. Eating breakfast still wearing silk pyjamas, without standing out like an oddball. I've always wanted to do this and finally dared to today.
15. Vivo barefoot shoes—the only shoes that fit my deformed feet. Maybe not stylish, but comfortable and toe-wiggle-friendly.
16. My silver cuff, handmade in Port Isaac, Cornwall—a present from Martin. One of the few precious pieces of jewellery I haven't lost.
17. Contact lenses and glasses—two tiny, life-changing bits of plastic, without which I'd be truly lost.
18. 3B pencil and Muji notepad.
19. Ninja light travelling and all the things that make it possible, including...
20. All-in-one, sodium laureth sulfate-free hair/body/face wash with geranium and orange.
21. Flask of hot coffee for the next stage of the journey.
22. Green tea.
23. Crème caramel and tofu (not in the same dish) for breakfast.
24. Aromatherapy oils.
25. Raincoat and woolly scarf.
26. Goods of Desire (GOD) Made in Hong Kong t-shirt and comfortable travelling trousers.
27. Hair bobbles.
28. Red lipstick.
29. Casio watch—cheap, waterproof, with both analogue and digital displays, and it lights up in the dark.
30. Speedo Endurance swimming cossie that doesn't rot, Speedo goggles that don't leak or fog up, a nose clip for underwater antics, and a silicone cap that actually keeps my hair dry.

Here's to another year of things—and people—to be thankful for.

And, to top it all, here's to the joy of becoming a nai nai, and the overwhelming love I feel for my granddaughter, Phoebe.

Happy New Year, everybody.

The King & I

January 10 2019

Empire Hotel Reception. Hong Kong

When I was eight years old, I took part in the local operatic society's production of *The King & I.* I was the tiniest of the royal Siamese children. I had a devoted on-stage mother and even featured in our local newspaper. I loved the whole experience, and after all these years, the songs and themes from the musical—"Getting to Know You," "Something Wonderful," "Whenever I Feel Afraid," "A Puzzlement," and "Hello Young Lovers"—continue to inspire me. Each one still holds a message that feels relevant today.

As I sit here in the bustling reception area of the Empire Hotel on a Thursday morning, I find myself reflecting on the musical's central theme of love and conflict—one that, in many ways, has woven itself into the fabric of my own life.

Today is the end of our holiday. Martin flies back to the UK tonight. Lucy has just arrived, but she'll leave for Shanghai in a week. And then it will be just me again.

Our adventure in Vietnam is one I will never forget — filled with wondrous, almost otherworldly experiences. Yet like any journey planned at the last minute, across an eight-hour time difference and on the flimsiest of itineraries, it had its share of challenges.

I've noticed that travellers often share only their holiday highlights on social media. They shy away from the moments that test relationships. Perhaps it's the pull to present a flawless image. But I believe there's something truer, something braver, in embracing the vulnerabilities and imperfections. If I can let go of the pressure to present a perfect picture of us as a couple, perhaps we can both embrace our humanity more fully—be kinder to ourselves, and to each other.

Martin never questioned my decision to embark on this journey in search of my birth family. He supported my free-spiritedness, my spontaneity, my impulsive nature with grace—even though he knew those same traits could be double-edged swords.

Travelling together in Vietnam laid bare the intricacies of our personalities. We both cherish our independence and solo adventures. We both like to be right. And our approaches to getting from A to B could not be more different. Martin, ever the meticulous planner, always had a clearly defined route. I, on the other hand, lived in the moment—embracing detours, changing plans at the last minute.

Both approaches are valid. But too often, they collided. We failed to live up to each other's expectations. We bickered. One of us would sometimes storm off in frustration, leaving the other confused. The trip felt like a puzzle—full of beautiful pieces that didn't always fit.

It was, at times, like holidaying with a cargo of firecrackers that could ignite without warning. But after the flare-ups, the sparks would settle, and we'd find ourselves in a moment of calm again—like when we arrived in lantern-lit Hoi An, and everything softened into something magical. In Hoi An, we lit candles and set them afloat in small paper boats, sending them downstream in honour of our fathers. For a moment the river held our love, our losses, and the light between us.

A highlight of *The King & I* is Lady Thiang's poignant song, "Something Wonderful." One line has stayed with me: *"He will not always say what you would have him say, but now and then, he'll say something wonderful."*

Now, approaching sixty, I feel more suited to the role of Lady Thiang than the smallest Siamese royal. That could be me singing—if only I could sing—imagining Martin as the King.

So this post is a tribute to you, Martin—my partner in adventure and life. Thank you for joining me on this journey, for loving me through the highs and the lows, and for continuing to embrace the puzzling aspects of me, and of us.

Here's to many more adventures. And many more "Something Wonderful" moments.

With my love

Laura x

One Good Turn Deserves Another - Helping Winnie

January 8 2019
Fo Tan, New Territories

Today, I spent time with Winnie Siu Davies in her spacious studio in the New Territories. In addition to being an artist, sculptor, and teacher, Winnie helps Hong Kong adoptees trace their families. I had the chance to help her prepare for Open Studios, and I've even volunteered to help at her private view.

I love the synergy between us—the synchronicity in our lives. My time working in an art gallery in St Ives came in handy. Today I helped Winnie "rehang" her space—though that's probably the wrong word when you're moving heavy bronze sculptures! I also suggested rearranging a few paintings, drawing on what worked well at the gallery.

It felt good to offer something back—to use old learning in a new place, in service of someone who's doing so much for me. Of course, she might rearrange everything once I leave. I can imagine her doing that! Maybe she was just indulging me.

While I've been in Vietnam, Winnie has continued her work on tracing my roots—and there have been some promising developments. My application for a Hong Kong ID is also moving forward.

I'll wait to share more until I've had the chance to speak with my children. Lucy arrives tomorrow, and I'm already fizzing—like a tired child on Christmas Eve.

Maybe we'll do a joint blog while she's here. I've always dreamed of a mother–daughter project—a blog, a podcast, maybe even a book...

Who's Been Sleeping in My Bed?

January 11 2019

Hop Inn Carnarvon Road

Today promises to be a bright one—even if the weather outside is grey and rainy.

The presence of this person sharing my bed fills my world with sunshine.

I'm so glad to wake up next to Lucy.

The bedroom is advertised as a double, but it's minuscule—mostly bed, not much room. And now it's cluttered with stuff. Even though half of my belongings have already been hauled off by Martin, who is currently transporting them across the world as I write.

Thank you, Martin.

Once again, I've broken my own golden rule: travel only with what I can carry and store. *Again.*

At least we're not trying to function in an eight-bed dormitory. We have our own room—and a private bathroom, albeit one with a very noisy boiler.

Our first task today is to get our little house in order.

As I survey the chaos of belongings, I can't help but ask myself: Why do I have so much stuff?

There's barely any floor left to stand on.

I find myself wondering what the Dalai Lama would bring on holiday.

It's just one of the many curious thoughts that occupy my mind today.

Boats, Yau Ley and Bengal Cats

January 12 2019
Hop Inn hostel

Not every day in Hong Kong felt like a reckoning. Some offered sunlight, salt air, and just enough space to remember who I was becoming.

One of Martin's chief complaints about Hong Kong is that it's always grey and overcast. I used to argue with him about that—and today, I'd have won. It was more like a summer's day in Cornwall, bright and alive.

My generous friends, Robynne and Pete, invited Lucy and me out on their boat to Yau Ley, an island off the coast of Sai Kung. We feasted on seafood at a beachside restaurant that felt like a Greek taverna, and there were enough vegan options to keep Lucy smiling. It was warm enough to swim, and I was the only one bold (or mad) enough to dive in for a post-lunch dip.

Later, on the MTR home, we met Dobby—a huge, muscular Bengal cat, perfectly at ease underground. I'd never seen a cat on public transport before, let alone one like him. Maybe it was the universe's way of reminding me of Dorey, my snow-leopard Bengal back home. Dobby made Dorey seem like a tiny old lady. I wished I could have brought her with me—though she'd have caterwauled so loudly, she'd have emptied the entire carriage. Dobby, on the other hand, was silent. Strangely serene.

So, for now, I'll take Lucy as my travelling companion—quiet, constant. Her head rested on my shoulder all the way home.

The only downside of spontaneous swims is spending the rest of the day in wet underwear and clammy clothes. The chill settles in your bones after a while. But a hot shower works wonders. Now I'm warm again—

all aglow with Hong Kong's unexpected gifts—and ready for whatever tomorrow brings.

Chi Lin Nunnery and Michelin Street Snacks

January 13 2019
Out and about

Lucy took charge of the itinerary today, and just as well—I'd lost my laminated Hong Kong/MTR map. It had become my comfort blanket. I still can't quite trust Google Maps, or my own navigation skills, not fully. Just having that map in my bag gave me confidence. The laminate gave it an air of authority, of indestructibility. Two qualities I've long admired—and maybe, just maybe, they're starting to rub off on me. Maybe I don't need the comfort blanket anymore. Let's see.

Our first stop was Chi Lin Nunnery. There are places that send me into a frenzy within moments—Ikea, for example, where I feel overwhelmed and desperate to escape. And then there are places where, no matter how many people are around, I feel still. Like I'm standing in mountain pose on my yoga mat—grounded, open, and deeply alive. The beaches in St Ives do that for me. And today, so did Chi Lin. Its courtyards, waterfalls, ponds, lily pads, bonsai, rock gardens, and golden statues slowed my breath and deepened it. Apparently, the nunnery's layout is designed to reflect harmony between heaven and earth.

In Chinese, a Buddhist monastery is metaphorically called a *cong*—a forest—echoing the Sanskrit *Sangha*, a gathering of monks and nuns. Together, they resemble trees, growing strong and still together. So today, perhaps I was a tree rather than a mountain—rooted, and reaching. I was mapless, yes—but I felt grounded. The memory of standing there, breathing slowly among strangers, is one I'll hold close.

Then came Lucy's next brilliant idea: a Michelin street food trail. From Chi Lin, we made our way to busy Sham Shui Po, tracking down award-winning Cheung Fun. The queue wrapped around the block, and Lucy—unbothered—joined it. It was worth the wait.

Describing the taste and texture of Cheung Fun is its own kind of challenge. Glistening white rice rolls, bathed in dark, velvety sauces rich with peanut, plum, and hoisin. Silky yet firm, soft yet resisting—like the slipperiest ravioli in existence, though nothing like pasta. It's Hong Kong's soul food—comforting, strange, familiar.

I may be confused about how to describe Cheung Fun, but I know this: Lucy was an excellent guide today.

What a Feeling

January 14 2019

That feeling—when you find something you thought was gone, and it had never even left the room. My map is back. I know it doesn't sound like much, but it was the perfect way to begin a Monday. My old laminated Hong Kong/MTR map—my comfort blanket, my talisman. The sense of quiet reassurance it gave me, just knowing it was in my bag.

Maybe it's a sign. Maybe I don't need it quite so much anymore. Maybe the qualities I projected onto it—clarity, direction, durability—are finally becoming mine.

We're off to meet Winnie at a local Births and Deaths office, just around the corner from our hostel. She's done more searching, more digging, and there's a chance we'll learn something new about my family. She messages to say she's running late. "Take your time," I tell her. "I've waited a long time to find out about my siblings. A few extra minutes won't matter."

Maybe today, all the things that were lost… are coming home to me.

An Antidote to Disheartenment

January 15 2019

I have one month left.

One month to search for my half-siblings from my mother's side. My father's side will have to wait. This journey doesn't unfold in straight lines—and it would be so easy to give in to disappointment when things stall.

Yesterday, Lucy asked if I was excited as we headed to the HK Immigration Offices—the place for registering births, marriages, and deaths. I told her: "I've learned not to get too excited. It helps soften the blow when disappointment comes." I'm not sure that's a healthy strategy for life—but for now, it's how I'm surviving this part of mine.

On the upside: if you're a pining nai nai, this office is prime baby-viewing territory. One counter for records searches, fifteen for registering births. We were surrounded by proud parents and grandparents, and at least nine newborns. I gazed at every one. Some swaddled, some nestled in slings. Some guarded, others offered up to the eyes of strangers like a gift.

And I imagined my mother, holding me. Bringing me to be registered—though I was already three months old, long outside today's legal timeframe. I must've been lucky to be registered at all.

Winnie had applied to search for my eldest brother and two sisters. But the result? Nothing. No trace. The woman behind the desk told us it was common—poor families, illiterate parents, farmers—they had more urgent priorities. Still, it stings. Especially when the search costs money, even when it comes up empty. HK$420 gone, and nothing to show for it.

So—I needed a recovery strategy.

1. Notice What's Gone Well

Before I came to Hong Kong, I knew:

- My mother's birth name.
- That she named a man who wasn't my father on my birth certificate.
- When and where I was born.
- Why I was given up for adoption.
- The last known address of my mother in 1961.
- That I had half-siblings on both sides.

Now, I also know:

- I've visited my birthplace—alone, and again with Martin and Lucy.
- I've walked past the address where my mother once lived—maybe where I was born.
- I've seen the kind of hut she might have lived in.
- I've met Celia at the Social Welfare Department and confirmed there *is* a big file on my adoption—the one I was told didn't exist.
- I know where my mother came from in mainland China. She was born around 1919, married at 18. She was illiterate. Her first husband, a farmer, died of natural causes at 48.
- I am not her fourth child, but her *seventh*. She was around 40 when she had me.
- After my birth father's death, she lived in extreme poverty. A village Chief helped her—with rice, and with my placement into Po Leung Kuk orphanage.
- Two of her children died. Four survived: two brothers, two sisters. One of my brothers was also adopted, likely informally.
- My eldest brother is about 69. My sisters are 61 and 66. I know my eldest sister's name.
- My younger sister was once given up for adoption too—but cried so much, she was returned to our mother.

And now I also know, for a fact, something I think I have always known but didn't want to face. Just when I was starting to feel like things might stall again—Winnie brought news.

Bittersweet news, confirming my mother was dead.

Whilst I was in Vietnam, Winnie had traced my mother's death certificate. She died aged 78, in March 1997, of a brain haemorrhage in Prince Edward Hospital.

One of my sisters signed the certificate.

A sister. A name. An address. A doorway.

It changes everything.

2. Let the Love In

The messages of support have been overwhelming. I've had advice, and encouragement from strangers and friends, sparked by a Facebook post on the Hong Kong in the 60s group and Winnie's media campaign. I haven't found anyone yet, but I feel held. It's like a wave—of love, of connection—lifting me along, carrying me forward even when I don't know the destination. And all those who send me messages to spur me on in the feedback to my blog. Just, well, just… thank you. You'll never know how much it means.

I've started helping Winnie in a small way now too—passing along useful posts, helping other adoptees. It feels good to give something back.

3. Next Steps

Winnie has applied to the Red Cross Root Tracing Service, to reach out to my half-sister—if she still lives at the address from 1997. It's in a poor housing estate, the kind with a heartbreaking rate of suicides. Hong Kong holds both extremes—wealth and fragility.

We've talked about me writing a letter—my own words, translated and hand-delivered by Winnie. But she's warned me: not all reunions go well. Families fracture for a reason. Secrets are buried. Some relatives don't want to remember, or reveal, or re-open what they've shut away.

I must be prepared—for silence, rejection, grief. Even so, I want to try.

I've written to Celia again too. Now that I have my mother's death certificate, privacy laws may no longer restrict access to her file. I want to read myself what has been kept from me.

4. And Then There's This...

I'm applying for a Hong Kong ID. Bureaucracy, again—first I had to be approved just to apply. Now they want more documents. But I got through the visa process (on the fourth try), and I'll keep going with this too. Today, I took my papers to Wan Chai.

So yes—there are setbacks. There are heartbreaks. But still, I can say it:

So far, so good.

If you made it to the end of this post—I owe you a beer. (Martin) x

And It's Goodbye from Her

January 16 2019
Lamma Island

It's Lucy's last night tonight, so here's a quick guest blog from her before she disappears off to Shanghai tomorrow.

"I've been to Hong Kong a few times before, so we haven't done many touristy things this time. Mostly, I've been focussed on food—and finding out more about mum and her family. Mum and Winnie have the family stuff well covered, so I've concentrated on eating as much as possible. Yes, I'd say that pretty well sums it up. And...

- *Shopping*
- *Gallery sorting*
- *Boat trip*
- *Ferry to Lamma Island*
- *Haircut*
- *Massage*
- *New glasses*
- *Markets*
- *Old Kowloon Walled City*
- *Dim sum (oh yes, food)*
- *Norman the Snowman at the Space Centre*
- *Watching tai chi in Kowloon Park*
- *Getting a tattoo*
- *Chi Lin Nunnery*
- *Sai Kung*
- *Michelin street FOOD*
- *Walking and more walking"*

Oh, I'm going to so miss her. Zàijiàn, Lucy.

Almost Local

January 17 2019
Kowloon Park

It was 21 degrees today with clear blue skies. I was walking to Kowloon Park—just five minutes from the hostel—for my daily swim. People are beginning to recognise me and speak to me in Cantonese. I felt a flicker of pride and excitement when I finally realised that what they'd been saying each day was simply "hello."

It was sunny and hot, so I took an impromptu lie-down to sunbathe in the park, thinking about how I was beginning to feel less like a tourist and more like a local.

The other day, I helped a woman on the MTR. She kept repeating "Kowloon Tong" and seemed unsure how to get there, peering at the maps and signs through a series of different spectacles, none of which seemed to help. I took her arm—I was heading that way—and she didn't resist. We got there without a hitch. She thanked me in Cantonese. Progress indeed.

I think being a tourist is a lot like a child learning to navigate the world. At first, I was dependent—like a toddler—needing others to guide me through each step. Then came independence: finding my own way, making choices without needing help. Now I'm discovering interdependence, where I can stand on my own and also offer help to others—even here, in my birthplace. Tonight, I was invited to a conference on the seven core issues of adoption. I offered a positive psychology take on the model, which some adoptive parents said they found reassuring. It felt strange—but good—to take part in the conversation while wearing several hats: as an 'older' adoptee, as a professional, a parent, a current root-tracer, and now, a grandparent.

Of course, while I might kid myself I'm becoming a local, it's *blatantly* obvious I'm not. Even on what felt like a summer's day to me, everyone—and I mean *everyone*, except the odd Westerner—was wrapped up in winter coats, jumpers, scarves, boots, and hats. Not a bare arm in sight...

Except mine, I'm in shorts and a T-shirt.

Also, proper locals know that lying down in the park is NOT permitted.

As do I—*now*.

A park guard came over, prodded me awake, told me off, and made me sit up.

Still, I'm content with this current state of play—both feet in several camps, being gently licked into shape by officious officials. I keep wondering how much Cantonese I could learn in the next four weeks. I'm happy to be getting on with my root tracing, too—more on that later.

Everyone is getting ready for Chinese New Year. There's a definite frisson in the air, everywhere you go. Apparently the city slows almost to a halt—transport, shops, small businesses, all shutting down. I need to get some proper local intel about how this works and when the closures start and end... otherwise, I might find myself a very hungry tourist for a week or more.

At reception, they said: make a lucky New Year wish.

I made three. For good food (Lucy would approve), language, and the courage to keep going with my search.

Serious Scribbling

January 18 2019
Hop Inn Mody

"You're always scribbling bits of stuff," says Martin. "You should write a book."

I try to hear the word *scribbling* with affection now, rather than take it as a criticism. My scribbles are not waste but work—the quiet part of writing that makes the rest possible. Like the virtuoso performance, carried by hours of scales no one claps for. Like the marathon, carried by months of training no one cheers. Writing doesn't just arrive, polished. It needs its scribbles first.

A lot of scribbling has to be done before anyone is allowed to read a finished piece. Today, I've never been more grateful for my scribbling—or for my attempt to keep this blog going. It began as a way to document the journey. But it functions on many levels. It keeps friends and family updated, helps me process and order my thoughts, and prompts the next steps in my search for my birth family. It also forces me to write every day to a standard that's good enough—for now—and that I'm willing to share. It's a delicate balance. It would be easy to lose focus on the root tracing and fall into fine-tuning blog posts instead. And today, I have three other pieces of writing that matter just as much.

A) A very important bit of scribbling – a letter introducing myself to my half-sister. Aside from today's blog, this might be the trickiest thing I've ever written: a simple letter to a half-sister I've never met. A person I may never meet. Someone who may or may not even know I exist. How do I write with empathy? Even if she knows about me, it will still be a shock to learn I'm here in Hong Kong, hoping to meet her. How do I offer just enough information? It's likely I know things she doesn't. But I also need to give her enough to prove I'm not a scammer—apparently, that does happen. How do I make sure she understands there's no shame attached to her, or to our mother's story? There's still a common assumption that babies given up for adoption came from mothers who were prostitutes—sometimes softened in language as "dancing girls." Families close ranks to hide this shame. In her own statement, my mother mentions three men: her first husband who died, my father, and the man she was cohabiting with on the night of my birth after my father had abandoned her. If my sister knows this and feels ashamed, she may choose not to meet me. Can I write a letter that might persuade her?

B) Another bit of important scribbling – a letter to International Social Services. To try and get help. After two meetings with the Social Welfare Department's Adoption Unit, I still don't have full access to the file on my own adoption case. The file contains information that no one else wants or needs—but that belongs to me. For now, I'm only allowed to hear small extracts, read aloud by a social worker. One extract described my mother's 16'x16' hut: dirty and unkempt. Two sisters outside—one rosy-cheeked, the other in rags. Chickens in the corner. And more importantly, a paragraph describing how my mother, from her hospital bed, asked to visit me in the orphanage before returning to mainland China to sell a few things—likely to earn the equivalent of two pounds sterling. That file holds more stories like this. But it remains out of reach. Winnie says many adoptees have experienced the same roadblock with Social Welfare. You'll remember that back in 2004, my solicitor wrote to them asking for help with my root search. They replied saying they couldn't help, but sent a tiny photo. Winnie says that happened to another adoptee too. But because we were adopted internationally to the UK, another body was involved—International Social Services (ISS). One staff member from ISS had been instrumental in helping another adoptee find her brother, so I'll reach out. Result! An almost immediate reply from a helpful ISS Social Worker. She's going to see if she can intervene on my behalf regarding the SWD file, and also check if ISS hold any additional case files in their own archive.

C) Scribbling a pitch. My reporter friend from the *South China Morning Post* has given me another writing task: a pitch. She wants me to tell my story just as I tell it in real life—natural, direct, no overthinking. She'll submit it to her editor to see if they'll greenlight a feature.

I keep thinking of Margaret Atwood's wise words:
"Your words are your voice, and your voice is like your fingerprints. Everyone's fingerprints are human, but no two sets are identical. No one else has a voice that is exactly like yours. Tell the page your story. Set your voice down on it. The page is very discreet: it won't pass your story on until you allow it to, so you can tell it anything, without fear."

Thank heavens for Margaret. And thank heavens for scribbling. Now… where did I put my 3B pencil and notepad?

There Is Such a Thing as a Free Lunch

January 20 2019
Indian Restaurant Hong Kong

A quick shout-out to the Anjappar Chettinad Indian Restaurant.

After a late swim that finished at 10 p.m., I didn't feel like trying to concoct dinner using just a microwave and kettle, so I headed out to eat. I had one HK$100 note—about a tenner—and wandered past Chinese dim sum houses, noodle cafés, rice stalls, and street food vendors.

Because what I really craved was Indian food.

And then I saw it: a few doors down from the Hop Inn hostel, a small, steamy-glassed doorway with a flickering neon sign—Anjappar Chettinad Restaurant. Inside, the clatter of steel trays, the warm glow of turmeric-yellow walls, and the unmistakable aroma of cardamom and cumin pulled me in like a magnet. I ordered a vegetable biriyani—one of the few dishes within my budget. But a few minutes later, the waitress returned, apologetic: they'd run out of biriyani for the night.

I asked if my $100 would cover a saag paneer and rice. It's my favourite—spinach and cheese, warm and earthy—and the dish Tom, Lucy, and I always order when we eat out at an Indian. We must have tried a hundred versions over the years. Maybe I wasn't just craving curry—I wanted a taste of home.

"Yes, yes," said the young waitress. And ten minutes later, my dinner arrived.

It turned out to be tofu instead of paneer—but still delicious. The rice was fragrant with kaffir lime leaves, cumin seeds, and cashew nuts. The portions were generous—enough for two. But after 20 lengths in the pool, I was hungry and polished it off.

When it was time to pay, the waiter refused to take my money.

"It's complimentary," he said. "From our restaurant."

Whatever the reason, it was an unexpected and beautiful gesture. Even without the free meal, I would have returned—the food was *that* good.

As I scribbled on the back of my placemat (with a borrowed pen), I noticed they have 77 branches worldwide—and two in London, apparently. Should you ever come across one, I can highly recommend.

Why Are You Here?

January 21 2019

Hop Inn Carnarvon

One of the wonderful things about staying in a hostel is the opportunity to meet new people.

Remember Agnes from Amsterdam, who convinced me to go to Vietnam? Well—now it's my turn. I've taken on the role of tour guide, trying to persuade Shane and Jennifer from Bristol that they should go to Vietnam too.

It's fascinating, the variety of responses I've had to the question: "Why are you here?"

Shane's answer might be one of the best yet—he just competed in the World Chinese Pool Championships in Qinhuangdao, a couple of hundred miles east of Beijing.

Shane and Jennifer shared a funny—if not slightly alarming—story about their first night in Hong Kong. They arrived at 2am and had booked a guest house not far from here. Shane described it as something out of a Hitchcock film—riding a decrepit lift full of rubbish and catching sight of two large rats scurrying in the corner.

Since Hop Inn was fully booked, they had no choice but to stay there for the night—at a *higher* price than here. Imagine their relief when they arrived at this lovely, welcoming hostel this morning.

This is Hop Inn Carnarvon. Its sister hostel, Hop Inn Mody, was my first base. Unlike Mody, all the rooms here are private—so there are fewer casual encounters. But the compensation? A lush roof garden. Having a roof garden is impressive anywhere. In Hong Kong, it's remarkable.

I find myself yearning to rush home to St Ives. Persuading Martin to somehow open up a bit of our apartment to the elements. Don't worry,

Martin—if you're reading this, I'm sure the fad will have faded by the time I get home. A few balcony boxes will probably suffice!

As I sit waiting for my laundry to dry, I can't help but notice the attention to detail in this place. There's a little cactus garden, plants rooted in recycled bottles and jars, and a wall that doubles as a guest book. There's unlimited free tea and coffee a, a hot water dispenser—and an honesty fridge stocked with craft beer.

An Apple PC for everybody to use. Fast Wi-Fi. Posters, artisan gifts for sale in reception to support local artists, and strong links with a community farm. The staff are delightful. There's a quiet sense of camaraderie among guests.

Oh, and let's not forget: no rats.

The hostel is adorned with art. A guitar leans in the corner, waiting for someone to play it. There's an extensive DVD library, books about Hong Kong in various languages, and a super-high standard of cleanliness.

I'll miss this place when I return to the UK. What I love most is the sense of community—and the small, thoughtful touches that make it feel like a home away from home.

And, of course, the chance to meet interesting people.

To ask them my most favourite question "Why are you here in Hong Kong?"

Tuesday's Child

January 22 2019

I'm on the Number 7 bus, heading to meet Winnie. Together, we're going to see her contact at the Red Cross—a woman named Bessie.

Unbelievable, really. Not so long ago, the Red Cross—and the HKSWD—told me they couldn't help in my search for my birth family. Back in 2002, I had written to the Red Cross, as they were well known for reuniting people, conducting root tracing. They replied politely but firmly: they were unable to offer any support.

But since then, Winnie, with her tireless dedication to adoptees, has forged strong relationships there—especially with Bessie. Since I first contacted them, the Red Cross root tracing department has grown. They now have a team dedicated to reunions, and Winnie's persistence has helped build a bridge to that team.

Today, we're going to meet Bessie—with renewed hope.

Winnie says there's a slim chance we may even try to find my sister today. But I don't really know what the plan is. It depends on what Bessie believes is best. I'm a jumble of nerves and excitement, trying to keep my expectations in check, knowing disappointment is a real possibility. Even so, I'm quietly holding onto a small, solid chunk of optimism—grateful for the progress we've made so far, and still believing my mother is guiding me home.

When Martin and I were in Vietnam, we stayed at a well-being spa. At night, instead of chocolates on the pillow , the staff left us coloured bracelets for the next day. Each night a new bracelet with a different word—love on red, gratitude on orange, others following. By the end of the week, I had a rainbow around my wrist and I loved it. Today I'm wearing my orange Tuesday bracelet. The word **GRATITUDE** is printed in bold white letters.

I catch sight of it now. A quiet reminder that even in uncertainty, I have so much to be thankful for.

We meet Bessie—and her colleague, Yuki. Both are warm, professional, and just what I'd hoped for. And more than that: they have a plan.

Later this week, they'll go to my sister's last known address.

But first, they say, they need to hear my full story.

I begin as I always do now, conditioned by years of experience to summarise quickly: "In a nutshell..." But they gently interrupt.

"No. Not in a nutshell. We want the whole story. Begin with your adoption."

I haven't cried once since leaving the UK—not even when I got knocked over by a scooter in Vietnam. But something breaks loose. As I begin to speak, I start sobbing uncontrollably. I'm embarrassed. I feel like a blubbering idiot, completely out of control.

But Bessie and Yuki are kind. They don't flinch. They let me cry. They encourage me to keep going. Winnie starts to cry too. All of us are wrapped up in it—the full, raw truth of what adoption holds.

At the end, they recommend a film—Instant Family—about the heartbreak and humour of forming a blended family. "You must go," they say, "and let yourself cry. There wasn't a dry eye in the house."

There's more on today's to-do list, though.

No time to pause. When I ask if we can stop for a cup of tea after the Red Cross meeting, Winnie shakes her head.

"We don't have time. We need to go to the government offices in Wan Chai—to check for your father's death certificate."

We head over.

After a long wait, Winnie receives two slips of paper. One for my file. One for another adoptee she's helping. Both slips say the same thing:

"No result."

Another dead end. Winnie expected at least some basic information on the other adoptee's case. But it turns out that she was adopted *within* Hong Kong, and birth certificates in those cases are protected to shield the identity of birth parents—who may still be alive.

I sit quietly, and silently thank my lucky stars. I already have a birth certificate.

There's one piece of good news. I've managed to persuade the International Social Services (ISS) team to let me view my case records—*without* needing to attend two mandatory counselling sessions.

Small victories. Small steps.

And today—something shifted.

A Different Sort of Roots

January 23 2019
Kowloon

Today was meant to be a day off from root tracing. A day to rest, swim, and soak up some sun.

I've learned my lesson—no more lying down in Kowloon Park. I didn't even *try*. Instead, I saved my snoozing for Hop Inn's rooftop. I fell asleep to the rhythmic hum of air conditioning units and woke up with a sunburnt nose. If this is winter, how would I survive a summer?

After swimming, I wandered through Kowloon Park with no particular agenda. Usually I'm dashing between government offices, ticking off lists, but today the day stretched open—and so did I.

I didn't expect to find flamingos. Or parrots squabbling in a massive aviary. Or a waterfall cascading beside a path I almost missed. I turned a corner and stopped still: trees like I'd never seen before. Gnarled roots spilled across the ground like dark ink, some rising halfway up the trunks as if refusing to stay buried. These weren't the trees I used to draw as a child—symmetrical, orderly, with polite little roots and tidy leaves. These trees didn't behave. Their roots climbed, reached, tangled. They seemed to say: *there's more to growing than going up.*

I once read that tree roots resemble the human brain—spreading out, forming networks, even communicating with one another. And there it was: my metaphor. I chose to believe that the trees' sprawling root systems were a good omen for my own search.

Later that evening, I went to see *Hong Kong Love Stories* at the Fringe Club. It was a joyful, hilarious play about the dating scene. Here, two central characters stumbling through a series of eccentric partners before finally finding each other.

I was mesmerised by one character—a selfie-obsessed Korean girl in a multicoloured bobble hat. The audience howled with laughter. At first, I didn't understand why everyone found it so hilarious. But on my way home, it all became clear: I saw a real-life version of the actress—posing dramatically in the middle of the MTR escalator, blocking everyone's path as she took selfies of her posing in an oversized neon-striped bobble hat.

Hong Kong's fashion is something else. Alongside the usual business suits, anything goes—the brighter, the better. Same with the cars. I've stopped photographing them for Martin now: fluorescent pink Lamborghinis, matte purple Rolls Royces, red Ferraris, a golden Maserati or two. Some are carelessly slung across pavements or junctions, as if hundreds of thousands of dollars mean nothing. It's as if status is measured not just by ownership, but by audacity. Hong Kong pulses with life, 24/7—chaotic, dazzling, and some unbothered by rules.

And yet, somehow, I fall into sleep. The city roars, unbothered by limits, pulsing with light and motion. But I drift off anyway, cocooned in the hum.

I remember a childhood game: rock, paper, scissors.

Could I invent a Hong Kong version?

Cars, fashion, roots?

I'm not sure how it would work—or what would trump what.

But I know what I'd pick, every time.

Roots. No question.

The Summit

January 23 2019
Kowloon

This is the summit. Years of climbing, of turning back, of losing the path, and still the climb went on. Until here. Until now. Winnie told me to keep the news quiet—tradition asked for silence. But I can't contain it: I've found them. My family.

After all these years of searching and hoping, the moment I've dreamed of has finally arrived.

It started quietly—with a simple WhatsApp conversation with Winnie about my Hong Kong ID. I told myself I wasn't chasing news from the Red Cross, even though I was aching to know if they'd found the sister who signed my mother's death certificate. But I'd learned to keep hope small. When you've had as many false starts as I have, you stop expecting too much.

Then came the message:

Can I call you?

Winnie never calls. She only ever messages. My stomach flipped. My hands shook as I stared at the screen. Before I could think I had pressed dial, heart thudding hard enough to hurt. Something was coming. Something huge.

"Yes", was the first thing Winnie said. "The Red Cross have found your family. They want to meet you". Then she said it.

"You have a little sister."

Silence, the walls closing in, as if they were listening. My thudding heart stumbled, and then seemed to stop altogether.

I once believed I was the baby, the smallest of both families. The truth was otherwise—and there was never safety in being small.

A younger sister.

My mother had another daughter after she put me in the orphanage.

And more to take in: the two older sisters I thought I knew? They're close to the little sister I knew nothing about. News has already reached her in Japan. She knows I'm here. She wants to meet me next week, when she returns.

And just like that, everything I thought I knew had to stretch, to make space for more.

When the call ended, I sat alone with my pounding heart. The adrenaline drained. And with it came the darker thoughts:

What if it doesn't go well? What if they're struggling—will I feel obliged to help? What if they don't like me? What if I don't like them?

The excitement is still here—but now it's edged with fear.

Then I breathe. I remember: every closed door, every unanswered letter, every cold silence from my adoptive mother... they shaped me. They built something strong. Resilience. Courage. A quiet fire that says: you've got this.

I stand at the threshold of reunion. And I'm ready.

I first wrote to the Red Cross in 2002. They said they couldn't help.

Now, 17 years later, I'm here in Hong Kong—and they're guiding me home.

It's as if the universe waited until I arrived in the right place. And then, everything began to fall into place.

On Tuesday, I'll meet at least one of my family at Red Cross HQ. I can already see it—the reception area, the red, black, and white. It doesn't belong to government. It belongs to humanity. It feels like somewhere I was always meant to be.

I don't have the right words for all this. Not yet.

It's still early in the UK, but I start ringing Lucy. Over and over. I need to tell someone. Finally, she answers.

Her sleepy voice lifts into shrieks of joy. Her excitement mirrors mine—but she stays grounded.

"Maybe there are even more relatives," she says. "Children. Grandchildren…" She's right. The circle will likely grow even wider.

But the moment I can barely let myself imagine is seeing a photo of my mother. Seeing her face. The face that is also mine. Will I know her, in the bones of me?

In the whirlwind of it all, I'm elated. Grateful. Still struggling to believe it's real. This journey has tested me in every way. But it has also shaped me. And now, I'm ready to step through this door.

Thank you for being here. For walking this far with me. This isn't the end of the story. But it is a beginning. A new beginning.

The one I've waited a lifetime for.

Old Habits Die Hard

January 25 2019
Kowloon

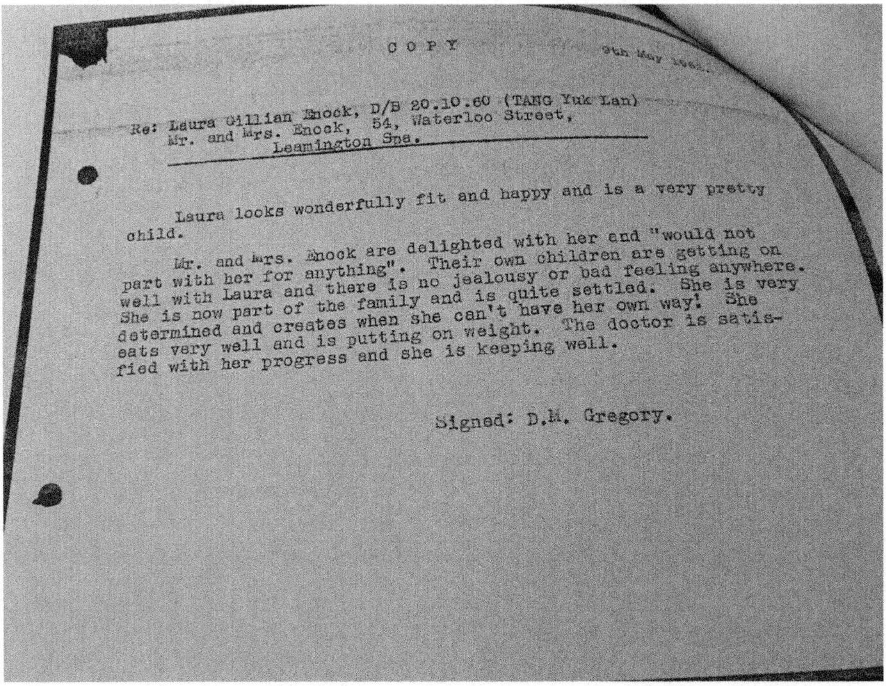

COPY

9th May [illegible]

Re: Laura Gillian Enock, D/B 20.10.60 (TANG Yuk Lan)
Mr. and Mrs. Enock, 54, Waterloo Street,
Leamington Spa.

Laura looks wonderfully fit and happy and is a very pretty child.

Mr. and Mrs. Enock are delighted with her and "would not part with her for anything". Their own children are getting on well with Laura and there is no jealousy or bad feeling anywhere. She is now part of the family and is quite settled. She is very determined and creates when she can't have her own way! She eats very well and is putting on weight. The doctor is satisfied with her progress and she is keeping well.

Signed: D.M. Gregory.

I got my file from International Social Services yesterday—and this line made me smile:

"She is very determined and creates when she can't have her own way!"

It seems even at a very young age, I was strong-willed and had a knack for finding creative solutions when things didn't go to plan. Some old habits die hard!

The file included reports from social workers who visited me while I was in foster care, and later, once I was with my adoptive parents. They make for very funny reading.

That first comment made me laugh out loud—and then this one:

"She hasn't stopped eating since she came here, and I can't find any food she doesn't like."

It's a bittersweet read. But the loveliest part is seeing the genuine joy my adoptive parents once expressed in having me.

"Mr and Mrs Enock are delighted with her and would not part with her for anything."

As you know, things didn't turn out quite as everyone had hoped. But it's heartening to see evidence, there in black and white, of a time when life was joyous—for all of us.

Lucas, Dangii, and the Art of Going Home

January 26 2019
Kowloon

Less than three weeks to go before I fly home. And bearing that in mind, every morning I look around at the stuff filling my room and wonder how I'm going to get it all back.

Apart from the H&M flurry, I can't begin to imagine where it's all come from—but I suppose a book here, a souvenir there, a few bits from Vietnam… it adds up.

But none of it compares to the sight that greets me this morning as I try to make my way through the common room to prepare my porridge.

Every surface is covered. An indescribable sprawl of stuff. Thankfully, none of it is mine.

Two young guys are wandering around, scratching their heads, picking things up and putting them down again, laughing and joking as they go.

Meet Lucas and Dangii from France. They've been living at Hop Inn for six months as exchange students, studying Business and Finance at Hong Kong University. After their studies, they travelled for a month through Myanmar and China—and today, they're trying to pack up their lives to fly home. It's a packing party in the common room.

These are the moments that make hostel life so unique. You witness scenes, share moments, encounter lives in ways no hotel ever offers. And for me, it's oddly comforting. A reminder that I'm not the only one who tends to accumulate a little too much stuff while travelling.

(Yes, they gave me permission to blog about their packing chaos. In fact, it inspired them to want a few snapshots of their own—though they couldn't find their camera. I'm sure it'll turn up eventually.)

Happy packing, guys!

A Couple of Firsts

January 27 2019
Kowloon

A few days after my arrival, on Sunday, November 18, 2018, you might remember I met up with Liz, a friend from my hometown St Ives. At that time, I still felt like a rabbit caught in headlights—no, more like a blind mole—tunnelling through the unfamiliar, nose to the ground, overwhelmed by noise, light, and the sheer density of the city. I struggled to navigate the streets of Tsim Sha Tsui, taking what felt like an eternity to get from one place to another.

Liz assured me I'd soon become a master of the underground, gliding through the MTR network from point A to B without ever having to brave major roads or battle the weather. I looked at her and thought, You've got to be kidding me. That day will never come.

I was wrong. Tonight, around 9 PM, I set off on a quest to find clotted cream. It was meant to be a small addition to an English hamper I'm putting together for some very special people I hope to meet on Tuesday. Alongside the clotted cream, I wanted a traditional Chinese New Year date pudding and to scout out fresh scones for the morning. English Breakfast tea and shortbread were already on the list.

Marks & Spencer or the City Supermarket at Ocean Terminal near the Star Ferry were the top contenders for clotted cream. I chose the latter, enticed by its exquisitely displayed global food range. With time ticking, I took the plunge and dove underground. Seven minutes later, I surfaced—right outside the Star Ferry terminal. A beaming smile spread across my face: I'd done it.

I know most visitors probably master this within hours. I'm 70 days in (though 20 were spent in Vietnam). Maybe I'm a slow learner. But tonight, it doesn't matter. Because suddenly, everything feels different.

Like when I slip in my contact lenses—myopic as I am, -17 dioptres in one eye—and the world snaps into focus. One eye for distance, one for reading. Monovision. The same city, transformed. Landmarks leap into place. Streets make sense. That's how it feels now—navigating not just Hong Kong, but this next stretch of the journey. I can see.

As I strolled above ground, shopping bag in hand, I paused to listen to live music and jumped out of the way of three boy racers roaring past in Ferraris.

I don't know if there's anywhere else in the world I might have a night like this. And as I walked home through this city that's beginning to let me in, I made a quiet note to myself to start thinking of ways to ease the transition back to St Ives.

With all the items ticked off on my shopping list, I convinced one of the fruit stall holders to give me a shallow cardboard box that I will decorate with red and gold. I stored my Chinese New Year cake and the English cream in the common room fridge, ready for an occasion that was once only in my dreams.

Earlier today, I met up with a new friend, Rachel, in Prince Edward. She has a studio and gallery space there and is not only a talented artist, but also a facilitator, teacher, and a member of Hong Kong Stories—a group of individuals from all walks of life passionate about storytelling. I had shared my story at a meet-up, and Rachel kindly invited me to record one of my blog entries for their station.

It wasn't live—thankfully. Rachel guided me through, offering small adjustments, coaxing me on. Within an hour, I had spoken my story into a microphone and out into the world. Another first.

What fascinated me wasn't the technology, but the way my words changed when they left the page. They carried a pulse, an urgency, as if they belonged less to me and more to the listener. Stories have always found their vessels—parchment, print, performance. This time it was my own voice, held in a recording, sent out in fragments.

Whether there will be a second doesn't matter. What matters is that I tried—that for a brief moment, my words found a way to move beyond me.

Blog Off

January 27 2019

In my bunk, Hop Inn Mody

Just for tonight I'm having a night off from blogging in favour of a crash course in Cantonese and some creative hamper making – all part of my hopes to make a good first impression on my newfound birth family when we finally meet. But rest assured I will be blogging tomorrow. See you soon.

A best of British hamper, cream and Chinese New Year cake are safely stashed in the communal fridge.

What Not to Put in a Hamper

January 28 2019
Hop Inn Mody

Proud of my creative endeavours and a little jubilant, I sent a photo of my hamper gift to Winnie, hoping for her approval. Instead, she reminded me that black is considered an unlucky colour for the Chinese during New Year, and that the sweets, being Japanese, carried echoes that might sit uneasily with some. Dark colours spoke of sorrow and endings, not celebration. So, following her guidance, I quickly revamped my hamper. The pretty gold tins, red and gold paper could stay, while the black-foiled Prosecco and the little cat-shaped candies went, hopefully saving the day.

I ate a few of the discarded black sweets for breakfast, half-expecting the sky to notice. It wasn't the wisest start, but I had been raised never to waste food, in a household where sweets were a rare treat. Then I set the day right with colour: the red of pomegranate, the blue of berries, the green of avocado.

As I plough up and down the lanes in Kowloon Park pool, I can't help but reflect on this city's paradoxical nature. Where else would it be unlucky to put black in a hamper but be considered safe enough to walk under rickety bamboo scaffolding held together with rope or nylon ties? Here, so many buildings sport facades held up by bamboo, underneath which everyone is happy to walk.

As I swim up and down the lanes of Kowloon Park pool, the rules blur. Black sweets in a hamper are forbidden, yet bamboo poles tied with rope hold up whole buildings, and people walk beneath them as though it were the most natural thing. I can't quite make sense of it—danger in colour, safety in scaffolding. The thoughts ripple and drift away with the water.

Today I let them go. Today I'll set aside all my muddled thinking about Hong Kong superstitions and step into the city as it is. On the MTR I carry my hamper of British delicacies, carefully chosen in lucky colours, hoping they will speak well of me.

A Real Life Daisy and An Album of Faces

January 28 2019

Red Cross Offices

This happened today. I met my eldest half-sister, Wong Yin Ling—Daisy. Real, alive, standing before me. Our reunion was a blur of hugs and tears, and I felt as if I had stepped onto a film set. Even the Red Cross volunteers—Bessie, Yuki, the others—found themselves crying.

This morning I woke knowing only three people who shared my blood: Tom, Lucy, and Phoebe. By evening my world had shifted. Two albums pressed into my hands, heavy with faces—brothers, sisters, nieces, nephews, children of nephews. Too many to name, too soon to place. For now, I will simply call them cousins to Phoebe. Proof that the dream was real. The family tree will keep branching.

Instead of the three I thought I was searching for, there are five. A big brother. Two big sisters. A little sister. And—yes—I've only named four, because the story doesn't stop here. Daisy and I have asked the Red Cross to trace another: my second big brother, the one given away before I was born. His adoption was not like mine. He was presented to a village chief with no heir, while our mother laboured in the fields, unaware her son had been taken.

Learning about my mother's life has been both heart-wrenching and inspiring. Born in 1919, she had eight children; I was the seventh. I had always believed I was the fourth of four, but today I learned I was wrong. Her first two children died during the Japanese invasion of Hong Kong. The resilience it must have taken to endure such loss—I wonder if a trace of that is in me.

Then came the moment I had dreamed of all my life. I held photographs of my mother for the first time. She was about forty-five, gazing back at me. For a moment I was outside myself, unable to believe it was real. Gratitude, sorrow, curiosity, connection—all flooded in at once.

When I embraced Daisy, joy lifted through me. It wasn't the teary *aha* moment of *Long Lost Family*, but something lighter, almost unreal—wondrous, floaty, as if I were moving through a dream. Yet even in that weightlessness, a shadow lingered—my sister far away in the UK, who under different circumstances might have been beside me, sharing this moment. I longed to say to her, *I've found them.* Instead, I held close what was here, careful not to let absence cloud the day.

After my adoption, my mother's life steadied. Four of her children remained close, a bond I am only now beginning to touch. Tomorrow I will meet them for a celebratory dinner, more history unfolding around me.

Today feels like the beginning of a new chapter. Even surrounded by newfound kin, I still hear echoes of the ones I lost—like a cloud across the sky. My meditation practice reminds me simply to notice, and trust the sky behind the clouds. Maybe that's part of belonging too.

My mother. Her life was hard, her circle wide, her love enduring.

My four half siblings

L to R. Younger sister Lee Yuk Lin (Ellen), oldest brother Wong Tin Fat, elder sister Wong Yin (Amy), eldest sister who I met today Wong Yin Ling (Daisy)

Family Jackpot

January 30 2019
A restaurant in Tai Po

In the photo above L to R: Willa Wong, my sister-in-law; Suui Li, my niece; Daisy Wong, my eldest sister; me; Andy Wong, my big brother; Amy Wong, my elder sister; Tim Wong, my nephew.

Have you ever seen a film where someone hits the jackpot on a slot machine, coins spilling everywhere, the crowd in a frenzy? That's how it felt. But I kept the dancing and shouting private, letting the reality sink in slowly.

The news had come just days before Chinese New Year—a holiday built for family, for travelling vast distances to gather, to begin again. My family brought the reunion dinner forward for me. I wore my new red H&M dress with a gold tasselled scarf—too much, perhaps, but no one minded.

I was "moy moy," little sister. Hands reached for mine. Food was placed on my plate. Hugs folded me in. They kept saying they couldn't believe it. My nephew told me he fell off his chair when he saw his grandmother's and father's names in print.

We laughed about the posters Winnie and I had put up. "That's how we find lost dogs," they said. My second sister walked past that very spot every day and never noticed.

The restaurant was alive with voices, waiters carrying towers of dim sum. Children ran between the tables. I watched, inhaled, let myself feel both the joy of being included and the ache of all the years I had not been.

When my brother realised I didn't eat meat, he spoke quietly to the waiter. New dishes appeared—mock prawns, tofu, sesame crisp. I tried to share them, but they pushed the plates back towards me. "For you, little sister. For you."

Later, he told me we would visit our mother's grave together. For a moment I felt it fully: not outsider, not guest. Daughter. Sister.

It touched a place in me that had waited a long time to be seen.

Even within the closeness, there were edges. Language danced around me—Cantonese, Mandarin, Hakka. I caught fragments, then stopped trying. Presence was enough.

"You're so little," my sister-in-law teased, "how do you eat so much?" I rubbed my stomach and managed the one phrase I knew. "我饱了 (Wǒ bǎole). I'm full." We spoke of future reunions, of the youngest sister still to return, of the lost brother who might yet be found.

That night I imagined my mother's spirit, watching quietly, delighted.

Goodbyes, New Year

January 31 2019
Royal Yacht Club

Everywhere I go, there are reminders that it's nearly Chinese New Year—red paper lanterns swaying, gold characters promising fortune, supermarket aisles filled with almond cookies and preserved kumquats. Just last week I thought I might be spending it quietly—maybe even alone. That didn't trouble me. I've always been fine in solitude. My main concern was the temporary closure of the swimming pool.

But life in Hong Kong has a way of unfolding unexpectedly. It offers more than I ask for. And now, instead of swimming laps alone, I'll be celebrating a traditional New Year with my newfound family.

Truthfully, loneliness has been rare here. From the moment I arrived, I was folded into something bigger—welcomed not just by the culture, but by its people. None more so than the vibrant, unstoppable Robynne Nimmo.

Robynne found me through a Facebook group and adopted me like a long-lost cousin. She took me on picnics and boat trips, bargain hunts and theatre nights, and once, unexpectedly, a hike that turned out to include a Bentley test drive. She introduced me to my landlady in Sai Kung, shared her family, her kitchen, her wit. Her one-liners are sharp, her picnic packing is an art form, and her generosity is boundless. Today, we shared a farewell lunch at the Royal Yacht Club—tasteful decorations, quiet harbour light, the kind of setting that feels suspended in time. She's off to Sydney for a few weeks, and I already mourn the space she'll leave behind.

When I got back to the hostel, the foyer had been transformed into a riot of colour—paper dragons, hanging charms, an altar of oranges and incense. No corner of this city is untouched by the spirit of the season.

As I prepare for New Year with my birth family and say goodbye (for now) to Robynne, I feel it: this sweet ache of change. I came here alone, expecting little. But somehow I've been handed belonging—in many forms. Friendships like Robynne's have lit my way. And Hong Kong, in all its noise and neon, has thrilled and captivated me—not as a tourist, but as someone coming home. I may be 58. But I feel, tonight, like a child again—eyes wide, heart open. I cannot wait to see what the coming days will bring.

Our Mother, Guiding Us All Home

A family reunited through prayer, smoke, and love

February 1, 2019

Mother's grave and back at the Red Cross offices

I never imagined my mother's grave would look like this: a huge temple lined with what looked like rows of tiny safety deposit boxes. Each grave was no bigger than a brick, holding a person's bones along with a photograph, birth and death dates, and the places that defined their life.

The temple itself resembled a tourist attraction, with coachloads of visitors, a restaurant, beautifully manicured gardens, and benches under shady trees. Yet, despite its scale and the touristy air, the temple was divided into distinct areas that created an unexpectedly intimate atmosphere for the hundreds of visitors.

The cleaning lady bustling around seemed well-acquainted with my family; I suppose they come here regularly and have built a rapport with her over time. She moved energetically, splashing water as she cleared away old food offerings and dead foliage. My family brought fresh food, incense, and flowers for our mother. I thought they would light just a few sticks of incense, but my brother lit an entire bundle—about 50 sticks in total. We took turns to kneel, foreheads pressed to the stone floor, incense sticks trembling in our hands. The red tips glowed like a small, shared pulse, while sandalwood smoke gathered around us, close and stifling, until my eyes blurred with tears. Through the haze of sandalwood, the red tips of incense glowing between our hands, I watched my big brother kneel, press his palms together, and bow low. His words rose softly, fragments I could not follow, until my sister-in-law leaned close and murmured the meaning: he was thanking our mother for returning me in time for Chinese New Year—the year that would have marked her hundredth birthday.

In the hush of incense and prayer, two monkeys swung down from the temple roof, landing on the low wall. Their red faces turned towards us. I felt the old pull—my lifelong fascination, the monkeys I'd collected and carried into children's therapy rooms, each one named and loved.

I half-rose to meet them, but my sister-in-law shrieked, tugging at my arm. "They bite." Her voice sharp with fear. My brother stayed prostrate, forehead to stone, weeping.

The smoke thickened, curling around the graves. Somewhere behind us, the rattle of a mop bucket. And then—bleep. Another. A third. Three phones lit at once: mine, my sister's, my sister-in-law's. We froze. I looked down. A message from Winnie.

The Red Cross has found your second big brother.

My sister-in-law bent close, murmuring the words in Cantonese to my brother as he stayed bowed to the floor.

Everything stilled—the smoke, the light, even my breath. As if the place itself had summoned the words. Then a second message: *You are to meet him this afternoon at the Red Cross offices. I will join you.*

My brother had been crying softly before. Now something split open. His sobs deepened, raw and uncontained—the sound of a wound breaking its silence.

Later he told me what he had carried for sixty years. How, as a boy, he had borne his younger brother on his back, delivered him to the village chief on their father's command. Twenty Hong Kong dollars. Their mother never knew until it was too late. He had carried not just the child, but the weight of that walk, step by step, through a lifetime.

The Red Cross arranged a meeting for that afternoon, three o'clock. My brother and his wife hesitated—they had a Friday art class to teach—but finally agreed. I told them this was not something to miss. In the photographs from that day, I am thankful he found someone else to cover the class. He was there.

Two brothers, face to face after sixty years. Their features altered by time but still recognisable. They held each other for a long time, as if to close the gap in their lives. It is one of the dearest memories I carry, alongside the births of my children and the arrival of Phoebe.

And yet, even as I watched, the old ache returned. They spoke quickly in Cantonese, laughing, crying, piecing together the years. I hovered at the edge—bridge, thread, question mark. I had helped bring them together. But belonging was something else.

Still, a thread had been sewn. Sacred, fragile, I trust it will hold.

This reunion marked the crest of my search. I hope my mother would be proud. In my heart I hear her whispering to Guan Yin, goddess of mercy: *Bring her home, my daughter Yuk Lan. Bring her home.*

The Shape of My Family. What I Now Know

With so much new information, I felt compelled to record and preserve how I got to this point.

90 Days to Find a Long-Lost Family

I embarked on a 90-day mission to find my long-lost family, arriving in Hong Kong on November 14th, 2018. Based on the paperwork I'd obtained from Warwickshire County Council, I believed I was my mother's youngest daughter, with an elder brother and two elder sisters yet to find.

But I was shocked to learn from the Social Welfare Department that my mother had given birth to seven children, including me, when she was forty. Her first two children had tragically died in infancy, and another son had been given away. This revelation motivated me to search not just for a brother and two sisters, but also for one more missing sibling. I also realised it was unlikely my mother was still alive, given her age and poor health when I was born.

With Winnie's help, we discovered that my mother had passed away in 1997 at the age of 78. Her daughter—my sister—had signed the death certificate, which gave us an address. We enlisted the help of the Hong Kong Red Cross Root Tracing Service and met with them on January 22nd to authorise them to act on my behalf.

To my surprise, just two days later, the Red Cross informed me—via Winnie—that my mother had given birth to another daughter after me. I wasn't the youngest after all. I was the seventh of eight children. The reunions began on January 29th, when I met my eldest sister, followed by my eldest brother, second eldest sister, nephew, niece, and sister-in-law.

After the emotional reunion dinner on January 30th, we agreed to visit our mother's grave together on February 1st. It was there, during our visit, that we learned my second eldest brother had been found and wanted to meet us all. That reunion was especially significant for my eldest brother, who had longed to find him for over 60 years.

Amid the joy and reconnection, I was also deeply aware that I would soon be leaving again—heading back to the UK, to the life I had built, while they stayed on, rooted in the same soil.

Family Summary (Siblings Listed in Descending Age Order):

- Big Brother: Married with one son and a six-year-old grandson
- Big Sister: Widowed with one son and a ten-year-old granddaughter
- Second Big Brother: Married with two daughters and one son
- Second Big Sister: Married with no children
- Me: Married, with a son, daughter, and baby granddaughter
- Little Sister (yet to meet): Married with two daughters (one of whom I have met)

An Extra Note

March 3, 2023
St Ives, Cornwall

As I reflect on this memoir and the journey of reuniting my two brothers after sixty years apart, I'm struck by how little I've written about the moment they found each other again, in the Red Cross offices.

Just recently, my sister Daisy sent me a photo—my two brothers playing table tennis at my second big brother's home, maybe a year after the reunion. There's something so quietly joyful in it. Two men, once lost to each other, face to face again, doing something as simple and familiar as playing their national sport.

In moments of self-doubt—whether as a wife, mother, sister, friend—I can be unforgiving. When I make mistakes, I mutter things under my breath: *Who do you think you are? Why would anyone be interested in your story? You can't possibly call yourself a writer.* It's tempting to give up and return to a more "normal," safer life.

But when I remember that reunion—what it took to get there, what came of it—I know why I kept going. I helped make something beautiful, unexpected, even miraculous happen. And that reminds me why I'm still here, why this story matters.

Today, I lit incense, as I often do, and thought again of that day. I looked at the photo of my brothers, heard the gentle *tap-tap-tap* of the ball, and imagined their laughter echoing through the room. The sound of reconnection.

That rhythm stirred something. A seed of a new idea: a musical, based on our family's story. Ping. Pong. The ball bouncing back and forth across time and place. A metaphor for my own journey, between Hong Kong and the UK. For our family—broken and stitched back together.

Once home, I dug deeper. I learned that my eldest brother's name had been changed from "Wood and Water Boy" to "Get Rich Quick"—a change that had obscured him for decades. No wonder Winnie couldn't find him.

What must it have been like for my eldest brother, carrying his four-year-old sibling through the streets, handing him over for twenty dollars? How long did my second brother cry, abandoned with strangers? I can almost feel my mother's fury and grief, coming home from the fields to find one of her children gone.

I've since learned that she was born into a wealthy family in Macao, but her mother gambled away the fortune playing Mah Jong. That she was abducted from a casino by an old man, used to ferry goods between Macao and Hong Kong. That she escaped as a teenager and made a new life in Hong Kong, where she met her husband.

When I finish this memoir, I'll begin writing a musical. The opening song will be called *Where Do I Belong.* A question my mother asked, and I've asked too. A three-act journey through her story, mine, and the long road that brought us home.

Trivial Pursuits

February 2 2019
Nathan Road, Kowloon

There are many customs in the run-up to New Year. This may not be one of them, but I decided to give it a try. The shops were stacked with face packs, each promising transformation. Why not? I didn't need miracles, but the promise itself drew me in.

The last time I'd tried one, I was sixteen. Mud that dried to cement, locking my face, muting me. This one was different: a blue sheet tucked inside a plastic sleeve. I smoothed it on, lay back, and let it sink in.

The instructions were in English. Around me, the constant hum of Cantonese. Should I keep learning Mandarin, or lean into my family's language?

When I peeled it away, the mirror told me nothing had changed. But inside, I knew I was not the same.

The days ahead would be full, crammed with things I could not do once I returned to the UK. I could always wear another face pack at home.

But what I needed here was the pause. To be still. To let it soak in.

Getting to Grips

February 3 2019

I am sort of, getting to grips with everything, including the following:

- With being with a large group of people speaking a different language from me, but sometimes talking about me.
- How not to make any more faux pas over the next very important days. Chinese New Year being the most auspicious time for families.
- Understanding who to give money in red envelopes to, how much is deemed acceptable and where to find an ATM that's not run out of money.
- Realising that as little sister, being told on a need-to-know basis, sometimes with short notice, where I must be and when is entirely acceptable. But never being quite sure whom I will find there when I arrive.
- Spotting when a sibling says, 'it's not important' that s/he really means that 'it is very important'.
- How the hierarchy in a traditional Chinese family works.

My head is confused. But I know that my heart is willing. As an independent strong minded woman in the UK, it is a huge shock to lose almost all my autonomy at such an emotional time and not to be able to understand most of the discussions around me.

I was told not to bring anything apart from my 'face' to NYE dinner. In case this is not what is meant, I've purchased some strawberries, white chocolate and dark chocolate and will attempt to melt the chocolate in the common room microwave, Bain Marie style. I hope to create something artistic. Imported Danish Cookies are very popular gifts, but I couldn't bring myself to buy something that is so run of the mill back home.

This morning, I met up with all my siblings except my little sister, and we took my "new" second brother to my mother's grave. His first visit and my second, all within a few days. So much emotion to express and so many feelings to be managed on the hottest of days.

And so much food! I'd already been taken to McDonalds for breakfast, and two hours later we all sat around a large circular table to eat lunch together. I felt loved. Secure even, as I shared the delicious vegetarian food that my family had chosen especially for me, in the restaurant of the famous Yuen Yuen temple where our mother is buried. I felt I belonged with my family. Such kind, warm hearted, beings.

MY FAMILY! Gentle, wanting to help me do everything, as if I were five again. So for now I'm going to be a well behaved and obedient little sister and enjoy these moments.

With all my siblings busy preparing for the holiday, I headed to Victoria Park to take in the Lunar New Year fair. The place was heaving—stalls crammed with red-and-gold trinkets, lucky bamboo, sweets wrapped in cellophane. It felt more theme park than tradition. I drifted through the crowds, half wishing I knew how to prepare properly—like a real Chinese person. Instead, I wandered like a tourist, no shopping list, no idea what to buy. There were some great Instagram shots to be had—if only I used Instagram, and if only I could take a decent photo.

There's so much more I could say—especially about the overpriced Donald Trump joke cushions: badly stitched, stuffed with lies, finished with reversible covers. Who would buy such garbage? Probably the same people who vote for him. But enough of that—I've got chocolate to melt, strawberries to swirl, and a mood to preserve.

My Surprise Little Sister

February 4 2019

I was the little sister in my UK adoptive family, and I always thought I was the little sister in my birth family. When I set off for HK on 14.11.18 this was what I believed to be the order of things.

I was wrong. Yuk Lin is my little sister! She is my moy moy in Cantonese, mei mei in Mandarin. I see me in her, and her in me. She is Yuk Lin. I am Yuk Lan. Just one letter apart. It feels intentional—as if, even after giving me up, my mother held my name in her heart and gave it again, not quite the same, but close. Close enough to say: 'you were never forgotten'.

Surprise Surprise, me and my little sister

My big sister, my little sister and I, all went on the bus to my eldest brother's house for what is known as the New Year's Eve Family Reunion Dinner. What a Reunion Dinner it was for us all. We couldn't have come up with a better title if we'd tried.

My second eldest sister was working, so we still haven't managed to get a photo of all six siblings together, but we did get some group shots to remember this very special day. My sister-in-law had put vases of sweet peas on every surface. These are my favourite flowers that my adopted dad grew at the allotment. The whole house was filled with the fragrance of the sweet peas and narcissi, reminding me of my childhood in England, in a good way.

I had decorated a Tesco's Finest cheesecake, as I couldn't get the Bain Marie chocolate dipping endeavour to work. I decided a frozen cheesecake would travel better on the MTR on a hot day and would thaw out en-route. It went down. I'd like to say it went down a treat, but I think my sisters and sisters-in-law loved the strawberry paper napkins more than the cake itself. Traditional Chinese desserts use ingredients such as glutinous rice, sweet bean pastes and agar—sadly none of which are in a Tesco's Finest cheesecake.

I only have 3 more days of celebrations left. One day is where I go, with my family, to The Lam Tsuen Wishing Tree, a popular shrine in Hong Kong. There, as is the custom, I will hurl a wish, attached to an orange, in the hope that it stays in the branches so it will come true this year. But what more is there that I could possibly wish for?

Wishing I Could Be an Angel

February 5, 2019
Tai Po. The flat where my mother once lived.
Kung Hei Fat Choy
Zhu Ni Xinnian Kuai Le
Happy New Year (of the pig)

It's late, and I want to remember. The day's been full, layered, joyful, messy—the kind that tugs at memory and deserves to be written down, even if imperfectly. And I've found something I might wish for at the Wishing Tree.

This morning, with the pool shut for New Year, I ran through Kowloon Park instead—reluctant at first, but grateful by the end. At the final stretch, I crossed paths with a Tai Chi master from Sydney. I'd meant to join the daily practice circle for weeks, but life—and our Vietnam trip—got in the way. Today, though, I received a spontaneous Qi Gong-style warm-up: fifteen minutes of precise, flowing movement. It was grounding and invigorating all at once. I'll be weaving this into my mornings from now on—a small new ritual from an unexpected teacher.

Later, on the MTR coming home from my eldest sister's flat in Tai Po, I met a five-year-old girl called Angel. Bright, bilingual, and bursting with questions about dinosaurs, the musical Frozen, and the science of condensation—in her second language, English. There's nothing like a chatty five-year-old to make you wish you'd kept up your Mandarin.

I remember when I was about eight, my dad made me a pair of stilts. Not the baked bean can and string kind, but sturdy wooden ones that came up behind my shoulders. I got quite proficient—I could even go up and down the steps in our back garden. I was wishing I'd kept them when I joined the tightly packed throng at the Cathay New Year Parade in Tsim Sha Tsui. I don't often lament being short, and I must be average height here (all my HK H&M clothes fit perfectly), but somehow I got squished behind the tallest and widest Chinese man in Christendom. He had a huge camera with the longest lens imaginable, and when he wasn't filming, he held it at an angle that completely blocked my view. The only upside was that I could see some of the parade on the large screen of his camera. Still, it wasn't quite the vantage point I had planned. "Why didn't you just move?" I can hear you ask. But honestly, once I was wedged in, it was like Chinese sardines. No going forwards, backwards or sideways until the parade was over. Not an experience for the faint-hearted or the claustrophobic. I think next time I'll watch from a screen or book an actual seat. *Next time?* Freudian slip?

I spent the best part of the day—and it really was the best part—with my family. My eldest sister lives in a tiny flat, the one where my mother lived. I loved breathing in that space. Seeing the tiny bed she slept on. My eldest brother lived there for a while too, and my nephew.

I've never worried about entertaining from a small space, and maybe it's a Chinese thing. When I arrived, some of the family were seated around the table, some squeezed into the tiny kitchen, and the rest perched on small plastic stools. My sisters took turns preparing and bringing out food. There was my youngest sister and her husband and daughter, my eldest sister and her son, his wife and their daughter, my second eldest sister, and eventually my eldest brother joined too. More new family to meet, and names to remember.

Straight away I was given tea, soup, rice and tofu. At first I ate alone, and later others joined in as more dishes arrived. When my eldest brother came in, his food was laid before him just as mine had been. Prosecco was served in mugs, and the meal ended with a large chocolate cake—the only thing we all ate together. I loved this relaxed way of dining. I'm not sure entertaining happens like this in every Hong Kong home, but it worked perfectly for my family. No one fussing over timing, just a steady flow of food and presence.

After lunch we all caught the bus to Lam Tsuen, to the traditional and very popular Wishing Tree Celebration. Fishermen used to worship a tree in Tai Wo, asking the gods for safety and a good catch. After TV coverage a few decades ago, it became a New Year's pilgrimage for many Hong Kongers. On the bus ride, my brother told me how the original tree caught fire (or so I understood), and how the government repaired it with concrete, nearly killing it. Now there's a replica plastic tree. You buy an orange and a tag—this year in the shape of a pig—write your wish, and hurl it into the tree's branches. It must stay there to come true. It took me several tries, but eventually mine stuck.

It felt greedy to ask for anything more, after the gifts of the past week. My new instant jackpot family, who have welcomed me into their hearts in ways I could never have imagined. Strange and sad and lovely all at once to think that I'll leave them in just over a week, to return to my other small and wonderful family back home. Perhaps one day I'll introduce both families to each other at the Wishing Tree.

I had a wobbly day the other day, feeling emotional and unsure how to be a proper younger sister—struggling with the language divide. But as the days go on and I relax, I'm starting to feel happy and confident. Like all the new things I've learned in these past three months, everything gets easier the more I do it. Sometimes I expect so much of myself—to get to grips with all of this quickly and with no hitches. Is that even possible at 58? Perhaps if I were five again, like Angel… I'd be fluent in Cantonese in a year, and able to name all the dinosaurs in Hong Kong. Oh—and she knew about volcanoes, eruptions, and lava.

Perhaps I'll retract the wish I hurled into the branches of the Lam Tsuen tree, and make a wish to be five again.

Off to a Cracking Start. New Year Celebrations

February 6, 2019
Tai Po

New Year, new rhythm. I'm starting to feel the gentle pulse of life here—not as a visitor, but as part of the shape of the days.

The new siblings were all up to different things today. I went with Big Sister to spend the day at my Little Sister's house. My First Big Brother is in China on a painting holiday—I'm not sure if he's teaching or simply painting for pleasure. My Second Big Sister is working as a housekeeper, helping with a family's children. My Second Big Brother, judging by his WhatsApp videos, is having fun setting off endless streams of firecrackers in his village. The screen filled with smoke as they burst into wild, joyous explosions—all sound and chaos and celebration.

And me? I ate tofu. Got a much-needed kitty fix. Gave a couple of neck and shoulder massages. And somehow ended up leading a mini tai chi and yoga session for my new niece and her friends—gentle, slightly awkward, but full of laughter and stretch. These small moments, these shared gestures—they're how we start to belong to each other.

I guess not every day has to be monumental. Some just hum quietly with presence, warmth, and the soft thrill of being folded into a family's ordinary day.

Hong Kong's Camel Trail

February 7, 2019
Tai Mei Tuk

I've never seen so many bicycles. It's 23 degrees and the final big day of the Chinese New Year holiday. Families and friends are out in full force near Tai Mei Tuk—the special area just beyond my little sister's home. It reminds me of the Camel Trail in Cornwall, that old railway line turned cycle path where families meander in the sunshine—only here it's warmer, more festive, and buzzing with the sounds of New Year.

I'd already eaten, but of course that meant nothing. As soon as I stepped through the door, I was handed a steaming bowl of congee, a box of rice rolls, and a large, sticky glutinous bun. I'd already been on the MTR and had a lift with my niece from Tai Po to Ting Kok Village—and earlier still, I'd run the sculpture trail at Kowloon Park. So maybe food *was* in order after all.

What I really wanted was to sit for a moment and take it all in. My mother came to this area to help care for my nieces, Suui and Wendy, when they were tiny. Today, I sat in the same rooms she once sat in, hugging the now-grown women she helped raise. I ate food my little sister had cooked—dishes my mother taught her to make. The feeling was soft and full.

Before I left, I learned how to say *I am very happy* in Cantonese. It sounds something like *ngoh ho hoi sum.* A good phrase to carry—especially on a day like this.

SULLEY
Rilakkuma
Rilakkuma

All a Bit Too Late Now

February 8, 2019

I'm doing that thing you do near the end of a long trip—counting down the days by how much toothpaste you've got left. Rationing the shampoo, eking out the final sliver of the fancy soap I brought from home. Wondering if the contact lens solution will stretch far enough (gas permeable users will understand the anxiety—it's impossible to find the right kind out here).

I can afford to replace it all, of course. But then I'd have to fit it into my two already-full cases. There's a deeper truth under all this minor arithmetic: I'm leaving. Again.

And where exactly am I going? I say I'm going home—but where is that now? Hong Kong, Stratford-upon-Avon, St Ives? All three carry some piece of me. In all three I have people I love—family, friends, fragments of belonging.

Today I bought a new book: *Teach Yourself Cantonese*. My family slip easily between Cantonese and Mandarin. In simple one-to-one conversations I just about manage, though Mandarin's four tones are hard enough. To sit at the table and follow the weave of voices, I would have to step into nine-toned Cantonese. Daunting. Part of me wonders if it's already too late.

Then again, I'm not the only one wondering that. Back home, Theresa May looks like she might be wondering the same.

Still, today I have toothpaste. A little soap left. A fresh book in my bag. And a thought I keep circling: perhaps home isn't fixed to a single place on a map. Perhaps it's a mosaic of all the places that have opened their doors to you.

Bu Qu. 不去. Don't Go

February 9, 2019

It's the beginning of the long goodbye. Farewells to favourite places, borrowed things, and beloved people.

I returned the saxophone today—the one I'd borrowed so hopefully at the start of this trip. I didn't play it as much as I'd planned, but even just having it near felt like a thread connecting me to my musical self. A golden presence in the room, reminding me I could pick up where I left off, back with the St Ives Concert Band. A quiet companion, holding open the door to that part of me. After I dropped it back, I invited all the friends I've made outside of my new family to join me for a farewell sculpture walk. I sent a message that said:

"To get, you must ask.

To find, you must seek.

Good morning. I'm counting down the days until I return home. I'll go back much the richer—with a new family, and a host of kind, supportive, and encouraging friends.

Living in Tsim Sha Tsui has been amazing (thank you, Winnie, for the hot location tip). But it's also relentless—a sensory storm of movement, heat rising off the pavements, the unmistakeable scent of Chinese food drifting from alleyways and open-air kitchens. A place where the streets hum with energy at all hours, where crowds swell and pulse, and where it's easy to feel both alive and overwhelmed.

When I needed respite from city life. When I craved space or steadiness, I'd come to Kowloon Park. I've swum here, run here, watched birds dart through banyan roots, listened to tai chi breath, opera arias, and even eaten the occasional McDonald's Happy Meal.

There are sculptures here—some very Hepworth-esque (look up Barbara Hepworth)—that whisper of Cornish home. We'll pause by them, and I'll remember how this park, too, became a kind of home. Not the home I came from, but the one I've found in unexpected friendships, quiet paths, and open hearts. Tomorrow, Sunday 10th February, I'll take my last sculpture park walk. Would you like to join me? Not to say 'Goodbye, Laura', but to say, 'See you again soon, Tang Yuk Lan'."

I didn't expect many to come—it's still Chinese New Year—but as always, my friends rallied. Ten people said yes.

Tomorrow, we'll walk, laugh, linger. I'll probably well up. Because I'm not quite ready to leave—not this place, and not these people I've only just begun to know.

Bamboo Girl

February 10, 2019
Kowloon Park

My planned sculpture walk was unexpectedly hijacked—though joyfully—by Kung Fu performers celebrating Chinese New Year with a burst of lion dancing and martial arts. My friends and I stopped, drawn in by the spectacle.

Eight teenagers, two just visible under vast lavish, embroidered lion heads, flowed in synchronicity, their timing impeccable, bodies bending, springing, climbing atop each other's shoulders. The drums and cymbals thundered. The crowd roared. But to my Hong Kong companions, it was all too familiar. A bit noisy. A bit much.

We abandoned the walk and wandered until we found quiet—two shaded benches behind a golden screen of bamboo. That's when it hit me: *Bamboo Girl.* A name I'd much rather claim than *Banana Girl.* Banana Girl. Yellow on the outside, white on the inside. A slur, often thrown casually, sometimes with a laugh—but it stings. It implies that I've betrayed something. That I've lost my cultural roots through my own neglect. That my insides have been bleached.

But I never chose to lose my language. I never got the chance to keep it.

How different it might have been if someone had nurtured that connection. My Mandarin teacher, white and British, taught her adopted Chinese daughter to speak Mandarin. She named her daughter Shaosheen, honouring her Chinese given name, Xiaoxin—*little new*, carrying the promise of beginnings—and gave her the option to change it if she wished. She stayed in touch with the orphanage and her daughter's first carer. She built a bridge, should her daughter want to cross back "home" one day.

No one built that bridge for me—but it was a different time. I was adopted in the 1960s, when the complexities of transracial adoption weren't widely understood. The focus then was on assimilation, not cultural preservation.

My teacher's daughter, adopted decades later, was met with a different kind of awareness. The conversations had started to shift.

And now, it's my turn. My choice. So I'll build my own bridge. And I choose bamboo.

Bamboo is strong and supple. It bends, but doesn't break. It feeds pandas, holds up scaffolding, turns into clothing, cutlery, flutes. Even golden bamboo—yellow on the outside—is not white inside. It's pale green. Alive. Quietly radiant.

Yes. Bamboo Girl. That's who I am.

And that day, despite the noise, the missed walk, and the drifting plans, ended perfectly. We ate together to celebrate Winnie's 60th birthday, her Year of the Pig. Her husband Oliver's birthday too. They couldn't be persuaded to come back to the UK with me. But we marked the moment.

Plans changed. The route shifted.

But Bamboo Girl rolls with it.

What a Tart

February 11 2019

Tai Po shopping centre - a cafe

This blog is dedicated to Alex, Anna, Ann, and Paloma—tart connoisseurs and loyal blog cheerleaders. Your comments have lit up my days here. You've made me feel tethered to home, even while everything around me has shifted.

Today I met my big brother and his wife for lunch in the heart of Tsim Sha Tsui. He chose a tucked-away Portuguese café I'd never have found on my own, buried deep in a bustling mall. A soft amber glow spilled from the windows, a welcome balm against the strip-lit glare of the neighbouring shops. Inside: colourful tiles painted with roosters, chatter in Cantonese and Portuguese, and—on the counter—a tray of golden, glistening egg tarts.

Not just any egg tart. A Macau egg tart, rival to the Hong Kong kind, in the same way Devon and Cornwall spar over the correct cream tea method (for the record: cream first, then jam). Where Hong Kong tarts are denser, closer to our British custards, Macau's are lighter, flakier—more like the *pastel de nata* we swooned over together in Faro. Funny thing is, you can buy pastel de nata in the Co-op and even the Cornish Bakery. But none of them tasted quite like this one in Tsim Sha Tsui—warm, flaky, glowing with saffron yellow yolk. We ate them all together in Faro once—all except Alex, who missed out that day. This one was for her too.

It arrived warm, the top just beginning to blister, the pastry crisp enough to shatter. I ate it slowly. Reverently. As if it were the last tart I'd ever eat. And as I savoured that sweet, eggy bite, I thought of you all.

When I was little, Saturday cake shop visits were rare, golden treats. My family would go for éclairs or fondants—all whipped cream and frills. I, without fail, chose the egg custard. Modest. Understated. But deeply satisfying. Maybe even then, I knew that what looks plain might hold the richest rewards.

This tart brought that memory back—along with a wave of gratitude. For your messages. Your memories. Your mischief. For reminding me who I am, even across continents and time zones.

So thank you, dear tart lovers and blog responders. Here's to talking through mouthfuls—crumbs flying, stories spilling, always room for one more bite.

Giving What I Wanted

February 12, 2019
Po Leung Kuk Orphanage

When I'm on my own, I find it hard to stay fully present. My thoughts skip ahead to Thursday—Valentine's Day—when I fly home, or my mind drifts back over all that led to finding my family. It's easier to stay in the here and now when I'm with someone else. My focus can rest on who I'm with, what's happening between us, instead of the growing pressure to fit what feels like a whole room into two small suitcases.

Today I had an hour with SY, a four-year-old girl I sponsor. She lives in the same orphanage where I once lay as a baby—Po Leung Kuk. Founded in the 1870s to protect women and children from trafficking, it's still a residential home for children aged 0 to 14. More than 200 young people live here, just steps away from the luxury boutiques and high-rises of Causeway Bay.

SY and I played doctors. She could have played any game she wanted but chose that. I was the patient. With her Hello Kitty set, she took my temperature and blood pressure, gave me an injection, made me drink pretend medicine, then applied a plaster. She liked that I followed her instructions—sleeping when told—while she tidied the little room, carefully straightening all the chairs. Then she'd wake me, and we'd begin again. We did this over and over, until, near the end, we counted together—Cantonese, Mandarin, English—using stickers from my Moleskine diary. We ran in circles until we were both dizzy. She asked me to pick her up and twirl her and clung tightly when I tried to set her down.

Later I learned she's lived here for two years. Her older sister is in hospital and couldn't visit for Chinese New Year. No one knows when—

or if—she'll go home. When lunch was ready, I had to say goodbye. It was easy to be with her. Moment by moment. I hope she enjoyed it as much as I did. I hope—if the conditions are right—she's reunited with her family. That I don't get to play with her again. So many hopes. So many feelings.

I ended the day with Liz from St Ives—who, by some lovely twist of timing, has been flying between Cornwall and Hong Kong throughout the same spell I've been here. We met at the iBar on the 30th floor of the iSquare Mall. Over Suzie Wrong cocktails served in pink cheongsam-shaped glasses (which we paid extra to keep), we watched the sun sink behind the skyline. Later we took tea, served in delicate Van Gogh china cups. We wandered through Shanghai Tang, oohing and sighing at every elegant item, soaking in the last of our shared time.

I've escaped the looming chaos of packing to write this, but it's time to begin. Tomorrow, I head to my second big brother's home for a farewell lunch. He lives near the Chinese border, so it will be a long day. I'm hoping to start adjusting my body clock, ready for Friday morning in the UK, when I'll see another little girl, my granddaughter Phoebe, who's twice the age she was when I left.

There I go again, thinking about Friday. It's only Tuesday. And wasn't I just saying how hard it is to stay in the moment?

As I prepared to sleep, I found myself holding that hour with SY like a fragile treasure—because it was, in many ways, the most unexpected homecoming of all. That I could walk back into the orphanage where I once lay as a baby, not as a case file or a lost child, but as a woman able to offer something—a moment, a connection, a thread of care—to a little girl living there now. I had the time, the space, the training, and the heart to follow her lead completely. The play was about her—but it was about me too. Because in meeting SY with tenderness and trust, I glimpsed the kind of care I might once have longed for.

I could offer it now.

And I think that matters.

There's no undoing the past, but perhaps in that hour, something was mended.

One Last Time

February 13, 2019
Hop Inn Carnarvon

Wednesday evening. Hop Inn Carnarvon. Tsim Sha Tsui, Kowloon.

I knew it was coming—the last night. The final swim in Kowloon Park. The last time I'd type at this desk, eat Asian food cooked in Asia, shower in my tiny ensuite, make tea in the common room, ride the MTR. I knew it, but knowing doesn't soften the blow. It hits low in the gut—that unmistakable ache of endings.

And yet, there's comfort in knowing I'll be back with my loved ones tomorrow. Back on familiar ground. But this is familiar ground now too.

This isn't like leaving after a week's visit. I have a family here. Faces I can pick out in a crowd. People who hug me, look out for me, call me little sister. I no longer scan strangers' faces and wonder—are you my mother? My sister? My kin? The wondering has stopped. Three months here, and everything has changed.

I'll keep processing it all once I'm home: the stories I misheard, the ones I barely dared hope were true. That I thought my mother was sold, only to learn she was taken. That she loved dogs—but also cooked them. That she listened to Buddhist chants. I'm still trying to square the contradictions.

I'll hold her tiny ID photos up next to my passport photo again and marvel at the resemblance. I'll remember the places she walked, the temples she visited. That final lunch in my honour—nine of us orbiting our round table in a constellation of chopsticks, rice bowls and vegetarian delights. They gave up meat for me. They piled my plate with love, and I ate every bite.

I said goodbye to Winnie on the MTR. Her stop, one before mine. No drama, no tears—just a selfie and a promise to meet again. Here, or in England. How do you thank someone who gave you your beginning?

Back at the hostel, I packed with focus. No repeat of the lost luggage disaster from the journey out. I tucked the photos of my mother into my hand luggage. The search results. The precious bits of paper that changed my life. The Kondo method worked—chaos became order.

I'm wearing two watches—one set to Hong Kong time, the other to UK time. Straddling two worlds. I took a nap to trick my body into the right rhythm. Now I'll walk a little. One final lap around the park.

This is my last Hong Kong blog entry.

I did it. I came back. I found them.

And I'm not letting go of anything that matters.

See you on the other side. Of the sky. Of the story.

All Aboard Feeling the Love

February 14 2019
In flight KLM

Happy Valentine's Day

KLM gave me an empty neighbouring seat and a red rose. Thank you.

KLM and a PR Campaign Written Just For Me

February 16 2019
St Ives Cornwall

KLM, thank you. I had the most fabulous flight home.

It was as cheap as rice but felt like flying first class. There was a spare seat beside me so I could lie flat and sleep. And just beyond—a wide open stretch of floor space, perfect for yoga and mid-air unfolding.

A Valentine's red rose arrived with my East-meets-West breakfast.

And as I boarded the final leg home—from Schiphol to Birmingham—I spotted the most perfectly pitched PR campaign. Words that felt like they'd been written just for me.

KLM, I know I'll be heading back to Hong Kong soon.

Let's fly together again?

Start-up,
here I come

Big plans,
here I come

Family
reunion,

Hong Kong,
here I come

Back So Soon? I Return to Hong Kong!

I'd barely unpacked my suitcase in February 2019 when Hong Kong called me back.

In the stack of post waiting for me was a letter from Immigration—a summons to complete my Hong Kong Identity Card application.

It was the card I didn't have when my Chinese visa was refused. In Hong Kong, an HKID is more than plastic and numbers; it's the key to belonging. Banking. Library books. A life.

For me, it was something else too—proof of my Chinese identity. A small rectangle of certainty in a story full of questions.

The meeting was set for 29 March. I booked the flight. Hong Kong, again—far sooner than I'd planned.

Here are a couple of blog entries from that unexpected return.

To Blog or Not to Blog. That Is the Question

March 23 2019
St Ives Cornwall

Whether to keep a blog for this unexpected return trip to Hong Kong feels less straightforward than deciding if I need an electric toothbrush for twenty nights away. To help me think, I turn to my creative bible—Julia Cameron's *The Right to Write*.

"Writing is a way not only to metabolise life but to alchemise it… We are all works in progress. We are all rough drafts. None of us is finished, final, 'done'."

Her words remind me to write because I want to, because it roots me, because it's human. My last Hong Kong blog—ninety days to find my birth family—began as a personal record and grew into a bridge connecting me to myself and those I wanted to tell.

This trip is shorter, just twenty days, but no less significant. I'll collect records from Social Welfare, celebrate two siblings' birthdays, get to know my family without the bustle of Chinese New Year, meet nephews and nieces, ask about my birth father, and stretch my Cantonese. Yes, I'll blog. Smaller in scope, but with intention. Easier, in the end, than deciding how many pairs of socks to pack.

Happy Families

March 25 2019
St Ives Cornwall

The day before I'm due to fly back to Hong Kong, St Ives mocks me. Yesterday she played her weather hand, and, as if holding an ace, showed her true colours. Typical. I've been weathering gloomy days since my return from Hong Kong. It's been an unending stretch of dreary grey mists and relentless rain. The kind that tempts me to linger under the duvet well past my usual waking hour, all the time bleating "will this ever cease?"

On Sunday St Ives puts on all her finery. She's not going anywhere, but seems to know I am. As if she's saying "why would you ever want to leave me? Don't you want to stay here with me, your gorgeous Cornish Rose. No rain today to hinder your lofty viewing. Look outward Laura. Stop your gloomy introspective ponderings. See my award-winning creamy beaches, my azure shimmering sea and baby blue sky, perfectly smattered with soft and fluffy clouds. See all the people, their little silhouettes of black, the odd smattering of sou'wester yellow and nautical stripes. A small child squatting to dig with a tiny red bucket and spade. The stuff of picture postcards. See all these people who have travelled miles to this fine and safe harbour of ours. Even without binoculars you can see their little figures crisscrossing the shoreline, making their marks on the tide washed, expansive clean slate of sand. See the dogs, racing to and fro, in and out the water, wet dog shenanigans interspersed with random vertical bounces.

I was so surprised by my hometown's unexpected sunny demeanour, I ceased packing and cleaning for a precious five minutes, compelled to gaze out across the sea. The brilliance of the day cast shadows that danced, creating a double delight of picturesque seaside views bathed in dazzling light. I remembered a similar day sunny day in Hong Kong when I stumbled upon a hidden temple in the midst of the city with dizzying skyscrapers and frantic streets full of shoppers and workers. The contrast between the serene, sacred space and the chaos outside was striking, much like the difference between St Ives' recent perpetual gloom and this rare sunny day. Both moments, though worlds apart, felt like pieces of a larger puzzle I was piecing together about where I truly belonged.

Of course, I must ask myself why anyone in their right mind would want to leave this jewel in Cornwall's crown. Was the weather really that harsh, did gloom drag on so long that I felt I had to leave her and rush back into the arms of my new love. Hong Kong. Sky scraping dizziness. Heart stopping city. Babble of incomprehensible tongues. The city where I, a small town, city phobic, woman unravel and lose myself. And find me all over again. This strange and familiar country where I must take the MTR to escape to islands that remind me of my Cornish home, travel wider afield to gulp down fresh air and frown upon lacklustre seas and beaches. What madness is this? What attraction lies within a windowless 8 bed dormitory where good sleep seems an unlikely event? Do I really want to trade the promise of a perky Cornish Spring for a hot and humid, sticky all over climate, where the only respite is to travel by subways or head into the 'free' air-conditioned spaces where I'll likely become prey to Hong Kong's consumer madness?

Today, St Ives plays her winning card—the weather, a rare perfection begging me to stay. But it's not only about the weather. It feels like a game of Happy Families, the one I so often lost as a child, never enough cards in my small hands. Now, with grown hands, I lay down a full set, confident. Happy Families at last. My cards tumble from my outstretched fingers as I prepare to leave.

Mum, I'm Home

March 29 2019

Immigration Department Hong Kong

"Put your right thumb there," instructs the young Hong Kong government official. Her face is masked, hands gloved in white cotton. I can just see her eyes peering over the top of her imposing monitor at booth 45, where we're both seated—she, following routine; me, feeling like I'm on centre stage, awaiting my final pivotal performance.

Her eyes aren't smiling, unlike those of the cheerful officer in booth 48 diagonally opposite, who's processing another hopeful applicant for Hong Kong's Right of Abode status. But I'm smiling enough for both of us. I've made it to the end of a two-hour interview process, and it's looking good.

Immigration Tower is an intimidating place—49 floors, 181 metres high. I queued 15 minutes just to access the lift to the 25th floor. Uniformed officers guard the lift bank like soldiers. I heard a man once set fire to the lobby in protest after being refused an HK ID. These IDs were coveted before the 1997 handover and are still highly sought after—especially the permanent kind I'm applying for.

At my first interview, only three of the fourteen documents I brought were requested: my original Hong Kong birth certificate, my adoption certificate, and my current passport. This was surprising. I had been told to bring all the documents on a very long list—old passports, current marriage certificate, previous marriage and divorce papers, two versions of my change of name by deed poll, etc. After a failed attempt last November, I'd spent countless hours tracking down every document. Now, I have a paper trail of my life. There's nothing like an overzealous Chinese official to force you to get your 'document house' in order.

The official stumbles over Martin's surname—maybe that's why I'm Tan, not Pemberton. I'm told to head down to the 8th floor for the second part of my interview. Thank heaven for Winnie, who's with me again, scolding officers for speaking to me in Cantonese. I wonder if her protectiveness might backfire. A banana woman who can't speak our language—wanting permanent status. Bah! Thankfully, the process is devoid of personal bias.

On floor 8, we wait among 64 open-plan workstations. When my Chinese name, Tang Yuk Lan, is announced over the loudspeaker, I jolt. It's the first time I've ever heard my birth name spoken aloud in public.

Back at booth 45, the questions I'd rehearsed for never come. Just a few more forms. "Put your right thumb there."

I press my thumb onto the glass plate. Then the left. She tells me to relax. My arthritic thumbs struggle with the alignment, but we manage.

Next, I'm told to sit on a black vinyl stool for my photo. "Remove your earrings." "Show your eyebrows." I try to pin back my fringe but my eyebrows remain hidden. She hands me hair grips—it must be a common issue.

That morning, I'd left my eight-bed dorm in the dark, jet-lagged, makeup-free—not even my trademark red lipstick. It never crossed my mind that it would all culminate in a mugshot.

The flash goes off. Two tired, 'old Laura' faces appear on the screen. I grin and choose the one where I look weary—but so much like my mother.

So Kam Lai. Fifty-eight years ago to the day, you pressed your own thumb onto an ink pad. I doubt you smiled. You were illiterate, desperate, starving—signing the agreement for me to be adopted.

And here I am, bringing us both home.

Later that afternoon, I walked out of Immigration Tower holding my new ID card in my hand. Permanent. Official. Mine.

Adoptees Reunited

March 31 2019

The Salisbury YMCA Hotel Hong Kong

Did you catch the *Call the Midwife* Christmas Special in 2018? It carried a storyline that loosely echoed the true story of me and my fellow adoptees. Back in the 1960s, more than a hundred babies—mostly girls—were brought from Hong Kong to the UK as part of the United Nations' Year of the Refugee programme. That TV episode? It was about us.

A larger group of around 600 babies were sent to the States, with others adopted into different countries.

Five adoptees happened to be in Hong Kong at the same time. Perhaps it was only chance. Still, I couldn't help noticing—the island had gathered us together, if only for a moment.

One day I'll share more about the story that came before my family-finding journey. But for now, my focus is on reconnecting with my newfound siblings—and on standing shoulder to shoulder with fellow adoptees in this unexpected and beautiful reunion.

£8 For the First Chapter of My Life

April 5, 2019
North Point, Hong Kong

I finally got it—the file I had longed to read, containing the details of my early days and my birth family's circumstances. The file that the Social Welfare Department in Hong Kong claimed they never had when I first reached out to them in 2004. It held the key to unravelling the mystery of my past, including the names of my half-siblings.

Remember how I sat at the Social Welfare Department desk, trying to decipher the file? After two meetings and a heated email exchange, I finally received a message from the Department of Access to Information (DAIO). Attached was a bill for HKD 79—about £8. Once paid, the file would be released. The payment methods were varied, but I chose the simplest option: paying in person at the nearest 7/11.

Hong Kong is dotted with 7/11 stores, almost one on every corner. Step inside and you'll find everything from Haagen-Dazs to phone chargers, toiletries, newspapers, and wine. And, apparently, the means to unlock your past. I can't think of a UK equivalent—somewhere you can pick up a pint of milk, a phone card, and also settle the bill for access to your adoption records.

The battle to obtain my file had been long and draining. To find the final step waiting for me under the fluorescent lights of a convenience store felt absurd, almost comic.

In the end, I had quoted Hong Kong law to the DAIO, careful to keep my tone polite. I couldn't risk another delay. By statute, the files must be kept indefinitely and released to the adoptee conducting a root-tracing search.

It took a thirty-two email exchange. I imagine someone finally thought: enough, give her the file.

For most, this stage ends with pages blurred by Tippex, whole names and details erased. To fight so hard, only to be handed silence.

I was fortunate. Being in Hong Kong, handing over my birth mother's death certificate, even meeting one of their social workers face to face—it meant less was taken out.

I remembered how long ago, Warwickshire and Hong Kong had been in conflict—two bureaucracies holding my future between them, arguing over consent as if they owned me. What still shocks me is how hard it has been, decades later, to claim what is mine—a story of no real interest to anyone but me.

And so it was left to me to bring their fragments together, piecing both files into something closer to whole.

The story had already survived more than once: first through a fire in Warwickshire, then through the redactor's pen, then through bureaucracy.

Paper can burn, names can be erased. Yet somehow, what mattered remained.

Under the fluorescent lights of 7/11, I paid for my past with a handful of Hong Kong dollars. But the receipt in my hand meant something real: after years of searching, my file was finally within reach.

On an early Thursday morning, I made my way to Wanchai, the business district on Hong Kong Island. The irony wasn't lost on me as I entered the tower block housing the DAIO office, perched above the showrooms of McLaren and Rolls-Royce. While billionaires might acquire their luxuries with ease, my own priceless possession was locked away within those walls.

The DAIO office itself was less showroom, more fortress—a small barred window in a blank wall, more prison than reception. I signed the prepared slip that confirmed receipt of my file, slid it through the opening, and moments later was handed a thick paper envelope.

I didn't open it there. The corridor was busy, the air-conditioned lobby full of people coming and going, a coffee shop buzzing nearby. It didn't feel right. I wandered until I found a quiet corner of the building, out of the flow, a space where I could sit down unnoticed.

The envelope was heavier than I expected. Manila paper, edges creased, my name written on the front. For a moment I simply held it, afraid to look inside, afraid of what might have been erased. Then, slowly, I peeled it open.

Sixty-one pages. The first chapter of my life. My mother. Me, a newborn. Three half-siblings in a 16x16-foot hut with a rusty bed, battered suitcases, chickens pecking in the corner. The file had been opened in December 1960, when I was three months old, and closed in 1968, when I was legally removed from the care of my temporary Hong Kong guardian.

And there it was—my beginning, waiting quietly in manila, held at last in my hands.

Jeanette Winterson named not only the absence, but the way adoptees must invent themselves around it in Why Be Happy When You Could Be Normal? (2011). For years I thought I was only looking for my mother and my family. In truth, I was also searching for evidence of my beginning—the fragments of a first chapter that could finally be mine. I claimed the fragments. Not the full chapter, never that—but the long road to reach them, what a story it became, and it is mine.

Resurrection and Return

Easter Sunday April 21 2019
St Ives Cornwall

In Hong Kong I asked the same questions again and again: Who was my mother? What was my story? For years the answers eluded me.

Now some have come. Faces that look like mine. Arms that opened. A family that made room. Two photo albums, heavy with proof. My second visit was less about searching than staying. Birthdays. Ching Ming. The rituals of belonging.

And today, back in Cornwall on Easter Sunday, resurrection is in the air. I am not a Christian, but I know renewal. The quest has changed me. I stepped into Hong Kong with uncertainty. I return carrying light.

I don't know what lies ahead. But I know this: I will not let go of family, of resilience, of the dream that carried me here.

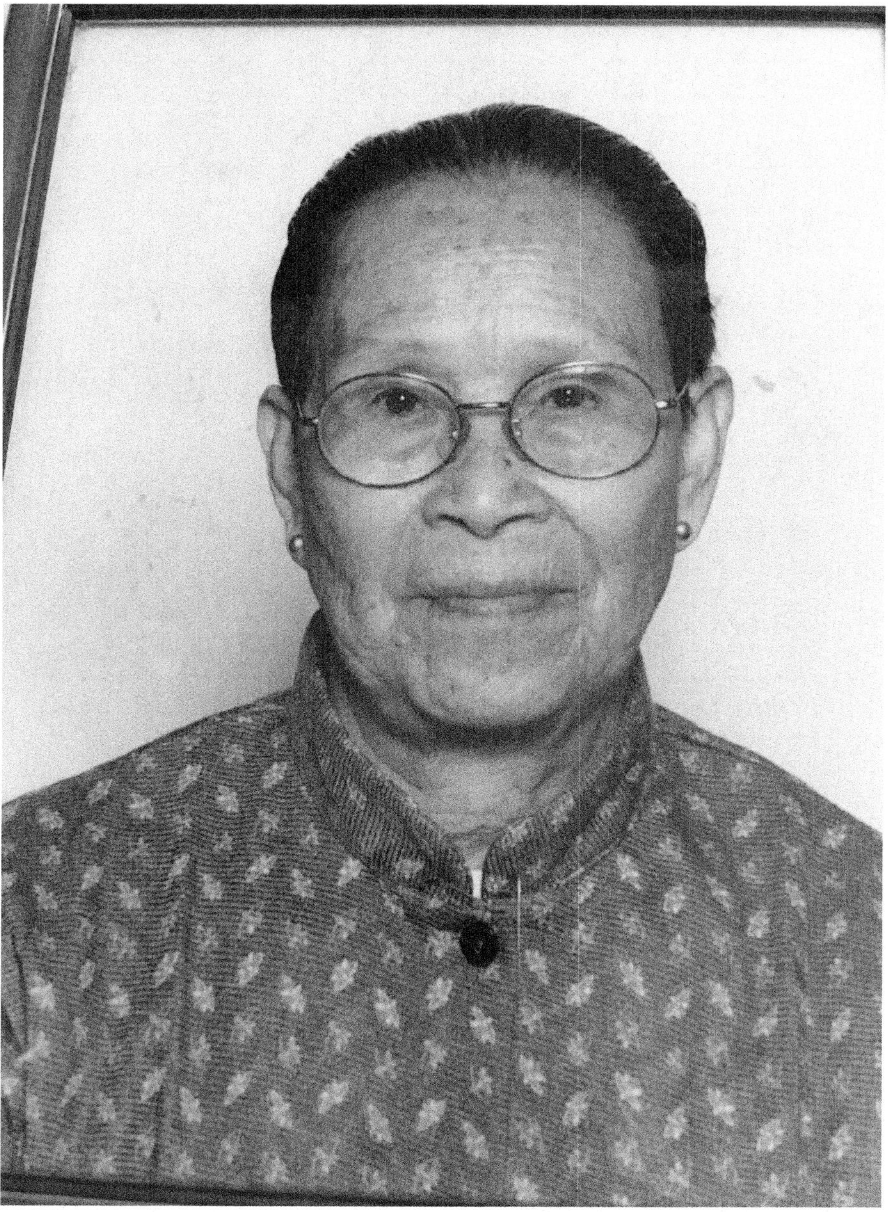

Photos: My son Tom and Phoebe. My birth mother, So Kam Lai
Goodbye Hong Kong

PART THREE:
Did She Live Happily Ever After?

What I found in Hong Kong was only the beginning.
The real search began at home.

Why a Part Three?

I could have left it there. And you can, if you want. Stop reading now—especially if you like your endings neat. Tied with a ribbon. Soft-focus. Resolved.

But life stories rarely end like that. And mine didn't.

I was high on belonging, fresh from Hong Kong, clutching my new ID like a prize. Home to swim again. Cornwall underfoot. Salt in my hair. Stories tumbling from my mouth.

I thought I'd returned a heroine. A kind of Odysseus.

Then—a scrap. Faded and confusing. Later, more paper trails. Odd, precise, dated. From the days I was pounding the streets of my beginning, trying to piece myself back together.

A shift. A shudder. A fault line I hadn't seen before. And suddenly, nothing felt solid.

The mirror held not the traveller, but a myth. Not Odysseus, but Medusa. Not the gorgon of storybooks, but the punished girl beneath the myth. Hair wild. Eyes wide. Frozen, in the moment the world slammed tilt.

This part of the story isn't about crossing oceans. It's about crossing a threshold. Into heartbreak. Into silence. Into truth.

I wrote the following letters in that quiet returning. To those I loved, those I lost, and those who I thought had failed to love me as they ought.

And in the writing, I began to make sense of the wreckage of me. And there, in that wreckage, I found something that had never left.

The roots I searched for had always been mine. Not planted in place or name but in the quiet, persistent returning to myself.

Here are the letters I never meant to write—and couldn't not.

Letter One - To Cathy Rentzenbrink.

As well as thanking you, the reader, for making it to the end of my tale, there are many people who deserve my gratitude—especially Cathy Rentzenbrink, author of *Write It All Down: How to Put Your Life on the Page*. Cathy gently discourages from referencing her in one's writing, but I simply couldn't finish this book without acknowledging her. Without her guidance, *Made in Hong Kong* would not exist.

I hope Cathy and everyone who supported and cheered me on during the "much longer than we ever thought it would take" process—feels my gratitude. I hope it brings them a little joy to see their names on the very last page of this book. There really is nothing like writing it all down.

Finishing this memoir has been one of the hardest things I've ever done. I regret how harshly I used to judge books—dismissing whole genres, rating low what didn't resonate, as if effort alone didn't deserve respect. I remember nights falling asleep mid-read, then blaming the book come morning, kicking it around the floor as if it had failed me. I'd never do that now. Every finished book is a feat. Dropping one feels like letting a newborn slip onto cold stone.

Now I understand the sheer weight of the work. An ocean formed from the sweat and tears of writers—and somewhere in it, a few droplets are mine. A mountain, built from the emotional rubble we sift through, sentence by sentence. I kept going—not in grand climbs or stormy crossings, but in the quiet, persistent act of returning to the page.

Even in lockdown, when the world shrank to four walls and worry, I continued. Though I had a lot of time on my hands, it was tricky. I was caring for my 90-year-old mother-in-law which, in lockdown, became more challenging. But the toughest thing I faced was beginning to write the memoir and then, part way through—at the end of 2020—

discovering that the years I had been writing about were nothing like I had believed, particularly regarding my life in the UK.

I had been living inside a version of my life I hadn't realised was being rewritten. The story I thought I was in had a second plotline—one I didn't see until the light changed and the pages fell open. I was no longer centre stage. The spotlight had moved, and I hadn't seen it go.

An African proverb says, "Smooth seas do not make skilful sailors." Life has gifted me with more than my fair share of rough seas, making me stronger and more resilient. Though not a real-life sailor, I've equipped myself with the writing equivalents of a sturdy small boat, big full sails, oars, a compass, and sometimes even an outboard motor. I've learned that one of the best ports to seek refuge in during a storm is the one where you drop anchor in a safe berth for as long as needed. You sit with your suffering and write it all down.

In *Write It All Down*, Cathy (who also wrote *The Last Act of Love* and *A Manual for Heartache*) "encourages new writers to open their hearts" (*The Guardian*). My heart had been broken several times, but even as it cracked open once more, I knew I had to somehow not let it harden and close again, become bitter and sour in the face of yet more adversity. In desperation, I turned to Cathy to ask her to mentor me. I knew that to continue with my writing would eventually be my salvation, but I was stuck and felt paralysed to keep going.

I've reproduced my letter to Cathy below. I like how it neatly summarises the essence of *Made in Hong Kong* for those readers who have jumped to these last pages. I'm sure I'm not the only one who sometimes skips to the end of a book.

The letter also encapsulates my belief that memoirists face a different set of challenges than, say, novelists. We must simultaneously reflect on our lives and wrestle our stories onto the page—while everything around and within us keeps shifting: the world, our communities, our families, ourselves, and our response to it all.

What we're trying to pin down often feels like a slithery truth, always changing shape in the light. One day we respond to a memory with compassion: the next, with fury or grief. We bring our whole messy selves and our many tangled stories to this painful, precious process. And if we can stay with it, work through it—then the writing itself becomes a kind of salvation.

My Letter to Cathy Rentzenbrink

Tuesday 8th January 2022. St Ives, Cornwall

Dear Cathy

For the last 24 hours I've been devouring *Write It All Down* and I thought, "this woman might truly understand me, and the way I think and go about stuff."

I live in St Ives, Cornwall and am looking for a mentor to support me with my memoir. Somebody who has walked their talk, who will support but also challenge me on my well-intentioned but haphazard endeavours.

My name is Laura Tan, or Tang Yuk Lan, or Laura Gibbs, or Laura Pemberton, or Penny, or Laura Gillian Enock, or The Said Child… I've had seven names and maybe because of that, I've a lot of stories to tell.

In 2020, I began my memoir, working title *Seven Names*, and was making good progress. Spurred on by being amongst the very first cohort of writers on an Arvon 'At Home' online writing retreat, facilitated by the delightful Helen M, whom I think you know?

The memoir's thrust was my tricky experience as a 1960s transracial adoptee, coming from Hong Kong to be embraced by a white English family. One of my Arvon tutors identified my story as an archetypal quest. A hero's search, in my case, for a family, culture, roots, identity, and belonging. Looking back, I was probably trying to cover far too much ground. Near-death from an accidental drugs overdose, expulsion from a scholarship-won private education, destruction of my birth records and complete rejection by my adoptive mother. These struggles likely contributed to the breakdown of my first marriage, following an affair. An acrimonious divorce left me riddled with shame and guilt, and as a M.A.T.CH. (a mother apart from their children). For as long as I can remember, I've yearned to put an end to all those tricky years. To stand tall and say with pride: "Despite it all, everyone lived happily ever after."

And I did. Reach that point. Momentarily, after decades of searching. After *Long Lost Family* (the TV show that offers a last chance for a few lucky applicants who are desperate to find long lost relatives) abruptly closed their search, I booked a last-minute flight to Hong Kong, bed in an eight-bed dorm, to return to my birth country to search. I gave myself 90 days. The outcome was mind-blowing and thrilling. One that nobody—not Long Lost Family, or me—could ever have predicted in their wildest dreams.

I was trying to write my own story alongside that of my birth family—a saga spanning a century, two continents, and the uneasy relationship between them. In Hong Kong, my birth family torn apart by war and famine but now finally reunited. In the United Kingdom, my adoptive family who were meant to offer security and love, tearing themselves apart, inflicting wounds that time nor death has healed. So many tales to tell, of love and loss, abandonment and betrayal. Stories of never giving up and the joy of forgiveness and reconciliation.

And so, I wrote. Even as I found myself alone, for a third time in Hong Kong at the outbreak of the pandemic in January 2020. Words ringing in my head as I voluntarily self-isolated when I returned to the UK. Later, in November 2020, more words that made little sense, landing on a page as I self-isolated again, this time mandatorily, alone again for a second time in a year. Morning, noon, and night I kept on with my 'scribbling' (my husband's not-so-kind description of my endeavours). All through those long weeks when we were all ordered to stay at home. Throughout Covid and Black Lives Matter, the simple act of writing kept me sane and helped me make sense of a local, national and international world falling off its axis.

But somewhere in the aftermath—when I thought I'd returned home to still waters—something else had already begun to shift. The shape of things, once familiar, started to feel off-kilter. A hesitation here, a silence there. I couldn't name it at first. Couldn't quite bring it into focus.

It wasn't until much later, after months of writing and unwriting, that I stumbled upon a loose thread. I tugged—gently at first—and the weave of my life began to fray. What unravelled wasn't sudden, but slow and quiet and strangely inevitable. I came to see that the narrative I'd trusted had been running alongside another, darker tale—one I hadn't seen, though I'd been living inside it all along.

I had been cut down while still reaching for roots.

The writing had stopped. A box I thought I'd long since closed creaked open. Out came the old snakes—abandonment, betrayal—not dead at all, only waiting. Their hiss was familiar. You are not special. You are not the chosen one.

But this time, I didn't run. Therapy steadied me. So did the sea. I sat with the old grief instead of trying to outrun it. I let go of the need to decide whether to leave or stay. I began again—not with certainty, but with rhythm.

In the stillness that followed, I reached for voices wiser than mine. Pema Chödrön reminded me how to live when things fall apart. The Tutus spoke of forgiveness. Esther Perel and David Whyte kept me company in the long nights. Clarissa Pinkola Estés returned me to stories of resilience.

I restarted a daily gratitude journal, and instead of chasing the splinters of a chaotic narrative that was never mine, I turned inward—to the jagged but honest pieces of my own story.

With friends, we formed a band—the Desperate Pioneers. I improvised on my saxophone, held up by others who forgave every falter. I reclaimed early morning swims and regular yoga. I cried through singing lessons, until the sound that came out no longer felt like shame. I meditated. I waited.

This was how I learned to stand again from the roots upward. Slowly, tentatively. Forgiving what I could. Gathering back the love that still existed for me and within me. All those years coming together to mend a heart fractured at the start—enough to salvage hope.

Enough to try again with what had come undone. To re-enter the ruins, not in search of blame, but to see what might still be possible. I began to understand that some things were always going to fall apart, not from what happened now, but from what happened long ago, far away.

"However traumatic a memoir may be, I think it's about love." I read Lemn Sissay's words as I came to the end of your book. Thank you for that quote, Cathy, and your encouragement to Write It All Down.

With your guidance, I am writing again. I know that through writing my story I have the chance to further heal myself. It is a sad and beautiful story that is, as Lemn says, ultimately about love. The love that begins when I am truly kind to myself—and forgive those who could not love me as they might have.

Would you mentor me as I begin again, Cathy? Thank you for reading.

Laura Tan / Tang Yuk Lan

Letter Two - To My Dad, Arthur

Dear Dad

I need to write about you, Arthur—my adoptive dad. In part one of my memoir, I didn't give you enough credit, and I regret that. You played a crucial role in shaping who I am today, especially after we reconciled. It was only after mum and Ruth turned away from you that you allowed yourself to get close to me.

In our family's tragedy, who were the winners and who were the losers? I feel incredibly fortunate—a gold medal winner—for having you in my life.

You, Arthur Enock, are the only dad I can truly write about. I still don't know much about my birth dad, Wong Tin, but when it comes to you, I have plenty to say.

In May 2014, after I helped you take out your false teeth and heard your plea to "let me go," and after the duty doctor told me you were fighting for your life and unlikely to win, it hit me: you were going to die, and soon. Your heart had seemed to be recovering well after the major bypass surgery, but now your kidneys and lungs were failing. You, your organs, and I were all caught in shock—racing toward a finish line we hadn't even seen coming.

Just the day before, I'd spent £20 on a prepaid TV card so you could watch your favourite shows. But then you were moved to a sunny corner spot in a quieter side ward, for more peace and privacy, and we couldn't bring the preloaded TV with us. We joked that whoever got your old bed would enjoy a nice TV surprise—and that we'd prepay another one, so you could catch up on *Pointless* while your body, along with some strong blood thinners, battled the four pulmonary embolisms that had finally been identified as the cause of your breathing problems.

You'd made a good recovery from the double bypass, but now it was clear that post-operative complications had taken hold, and you would never return to your beloved allotment to finish planting your seedling potatoes.

Your last words to me, as I removed your dentures, were:

"Thank you. You've been the best daughter I could ever have wished for."

Even though you only had one other daughter—your birth daughter, from whom you'd been estranged for many years—I tried to receive your words with the love and grace they were given.

It took too long for you to die after they administered the sedative and morphine. For two precious days and nights, I stayed by your side. I moistened your mouth with ice chips, stroked your head, and finally got to touch those big ears you disliked so much.

Over six feet tall, you always stood proud and upright, with a full head of hair at eighty-three. Your ears stuck out so much you reminded me of Roald Dahl's BFG. You cared about your appearance—even at the end. Before I reached your bedside, before they began palliative care, even as you must have realised you were ready to stop fighting, I could see you'd tried to comb your hair.

There was sad evidence you'd also tried to shave: small cuts on your chin, only half a moustache left. On the locker beside you lay your comb, safety razor, and a small mirror, abandoned. Appearances mattered to you, dad. Your ears were one of the few things you ever mentioned about your childhood.

You were convinced that if any of your siblings had ears that stuck out so terribly, your mother—my grandmother—would have had them pinned back. You believed you were her least favourite child. You carried the sense of a life barely welcomed, and her failure to 'fix' your ears became the proof. Had you been her eldest son, or her beloved only daughter, or her surprise post-war baby who could do no wrong, maybe then, you thought, your ears would have been pinned back. But instead they're listening still, somewhere I cannot reach, to every word I write.

Maybe Chris inherited that same "least favourite child" feeling. He once told me he believed you loved me most, and that mum loved Ruth best. He said he felt left out in the cold—that as a young adult, he'd brought shame on the family.

That's not how I see it. But I suppose that's the trouble with memory. Everyone looks back and sees something different. Whether Chris is right or wrong, the idea of being unwanted, the least loved—that's something you, he, and I all carried. A belief that shaped the way we saw ourselves, the way we lived.

And that belief must no longer direct mine.

So I'm making a stand. I'm saying:

I do count. I have the right to be kind to myself. I am loveable and loving. I deserve to be loved."

Writing to you has helped me see this. Not long after our reconciliation, you asked, "You had a good childhood, didn't you?" I nodded, said, "I guess so." But what I wanted to say was, "It was okay… but it would have been easier if you had protected me a bit more."

Looking back now, I can see how—in our strange little Enock family, it would've been hard for you to defend me when you could barely defend yourself against mum.

Dear dad, I know you did your very best, without good role models to guide you. I am learning to forgive you, and others, for not being there for me. Most importantly, I've learned to hold my own.

Remembering what a great shop steward and union rep you were, I think you'd be proud to know that now, sometimes, I even speak up for others too. You helped me rise to this place, and for that, I am grateful.

I miss you, dad. With all my love

Your best daughter

Letter Three - To My Mum, Cath

Dear Mum

I took part in the Hoffman Process alongside 23 other hopefuls, each of us longing to heal, stop hurting, and live more authentically. Hoffman is an intense week-long personal development retreat that helps individuals uncover and heal deep emotional patterns and wounds, enabling them to make positive changes in their lives.

As I read the lopsided rant of part one of my memoir, I realised I must still be dragging around a huge amount of anger and resentment about us—anger I stupidly believed I had put to bed long ago. I'd somehow convinced myself that the demise of our relationship no longer had the power to affect my life—that I'd forgiven, forgotten, and moved on. How wrong I was. The truth surfaced as my second marriage fell apart. I saw, too, that in my accounts of my early years in this memoir, I had put you on trial for being the worst mother ever. I had presented the prosecution's case and you were found guilty, without ever having the chance to defend yourself. Which of course you no longer can.

I had to find a way of releasing the weight of sadness and anger that was still dragging me and others down, still consuming me. I did Hoffman.

During the Hoffman Process, there was an exercise where my twelve-year-old self sat down with your twelve-year-old self and I asked you about your own experiences as a child. It was in that moment of connection that I finally grasped how difficult your own adoption experience must have been. It wasn't just a cognitive realisation—it landed in every cell of my body, as if something long-buried had finally made sense. It dawned at last, that the patterns and wounds handed down to you from your own adoptive mother had been passed down to me, perpetuating a cycle of blame, criticism and rejection. Patterns that I must now discontinue.

I was asked to bring to the Hoffman Process three items that reminded me of you in a positive light. Sadly, I have nothing of yours, mum, which speaks volumes. In fact, the only item I had was the order of service from your funeral. The funeral to which I was not invited—a painful reminder of the divide between us that carried on even beyond your death. Because I only had this, for the second item, I wrote out the lyrics to Clint Eastwood's "I Talk to the Trees," from the musical Paint Your Wagon. The song you used to sing as we dusted the piano together. A song about speaking and not being heard. It felt like us.

"I talk to the trees
But they don't listen to me
I talk to the stars
But they never hear me
The breeze hasn't time
To stop, and hear what I say
I talk to them all
In vain

Yet I also remember the joy of your voice filling the room, a rare tenderness, carrying me with it.

Our story wasn't only anger and silence. Sometimes it was music and light.

For my third item, I picked a perfect white magnolia flower from a tree in the garden at the retreat—a 20-foot tree weighed down with blooms. It reminded me of the 40-foot tree in the garden at Lanyon, the home you and dad restored together. Did you know that my name, Yuk Lan, can also mean white magnolia—as well as beautiful flower, or Jade Orchid?

During my Hoffman week there was so much healing and growth and new understanding. I am now proud to display that order of service with your photograph as a young woman, which pre-Hoffman I kept hidden in my filing cabinet. I see it as a symbol of my journey towards breaking the negative patterns that were handed down to you from your own adoptive mother, and then from you to me. It serves as a testament to the power of forgiveness and love.

Oh Cath, I regret that we never had the chance for a real conversation, but writing this letter makes me feel close to you, but it also reminds me of the distance that never closed between us. Perhaps that's the paradox: love and hurt, both true at once. Forgiveness softens me, but it doesn't rewrite the past. What it gives me is the chance to begin again—still learning, still growing, still unfinished. I want my children and granddaughters to see a better way of moving forward—one built on understanding, forgiveness, and love. But even as I try, I know I will falter. The patterns run deep. Still, I keep trying. That, perhaps, is the truest gift I can offer, not a neat ending, but a willingness to keep learning how to love.

Mum, if you were still alive, I'd try to find the courage to come to you, look you in the eyes, and say, "Thank you. I love you." But I'd also want to ask you things I never will. Some answers are lost, and maybe I'll always carry that gap. Healing doesn't erase it, but it teaches me how to live alongside it.

Laura

Letter Four - To Laura From Yuk Lan

2020

I was in the sauna today when a man told me about a memoir he had read. In it, the author began by writing about the life he wished he'd had—only to later realise that the life he actually lived, though grim at times, was ultimately better. I couldn't help punching the air and shouting out loud, "You know, I feel exactly the same."

Dear Laura

I, Yuk Lan, write to you from your future—twenty years from now. Maybe three-quarters of your life is behind you, with one quarter left, if you live to be eighty. But then again, it would be a very different ratio if you were to die tomorrow.

I know you aspire to achieve so much in the years to come, dear woman. You yearn to leave a legacy, to make a difference. You're always asking what path to take to become who you're meant to be. But who am I to guide you?

I am you—your past self, your present self, your future self. Whether you have twenty years, twenty weeks, twenty days, or only twenty minutes left, the wisdom lies in this: you don't know your expiry date. And no one else does either.

You navigate life without a compass or a known countdown. You in your small boat, trying to steer away from the rocks, seeking safe harbour. I see you, rowing tirelessly, going in circles. You feel elated when others mistake you for a lighthouse. You feel crushed when someone else's oar knocks you sideways, capsizing you silently, or pushing you toward the rocks. Exposing you to a tsunami of threat and grief.

But I don't believe death will come to you like that. Don't fear it. Instead, play with it—imagine endings. The final chapter is yours to envision. Picture this: a gentle wave tips your boat. You fall into the sea, half-asleep. As you come to, you remember—you're a strong swimmer. The water is cold. There are sharks. Wounded people are bleeding nearby. And the sharks are not interested in you.

You climb back into your boat. The sun rises, then sets. You fall out, flounder again. It's like a living death, night after night.

Then—on the horizon—you see another small boat. It draws closer, despite the pitching waves. Its sailor smiles. You can't tell if they're man or woman. They wear loose, sun-faded clothing and a wide straw hat. Their long grey hair peeks out, their face weathered. They offer you fish, bread, fresh water—and lobster.

Did you know, that when life becomes too tight for a lobster, when there's no more room to grow, it hides away and sheds its shell? Then grows a new one. This fisherperson has pots brimming with deep orange lobsters. They nourish you. They offer honey. They show you how to fend off sharks and take care of yourself.

But what will you sacrifice to stay safe? Will you feast? Will you free the lobsters? These are lessons you were meant to learn long ago—but it's not too late. You were a late bloomer, but lately you've begun to flourish. Feast, yes—but watch for the barbs and traps in the lobster pots.

My darling Laura. There is so much I want to share with you. I see you've made yourself a cup of *Love*—a Pukka tea. Wise choice. Now, sip slowly. Let the scents of rose, chamomile, and lavender steady you as you listen to what I have to say.

Don't settle for this moment of calm. Let it nourish you, yes—but let it also spur you to go further. To go beyond. And to go alone in your boat, even if you're sure you'll sink.

I hear your cry: a child's call for the love of your mothers—both of them—to come and rescue you. You long for a mother's omnipotent love.

You wail: "If only!" If only Mother A had not done what she did. If only Mother B had made up for Mother A's failings, instead of sending you off in a boat punctured with holes she herself drilled.

If only you had suckled on the milk of unconditional love—would it have changed everything?

I wish I could say yes. I wish I could promise that a perfect start would've led to a perfect life. But you and I both know, even with a cruise liner and a full crew, there would still be storms. The shape of the story might change, but not its essence: birth, life, death.

Some are handed a raft of twigs and sink without a trace. Some navigate solo. Some discover new lands. I can't tell you your ending. Only this: it ends in death. One day. One time.

You didn't choose the circumstances of your birth. You likely won't choose the manner of your death. But here's what you *can* choose, dear Laura:

How you live now.

If you can love yourself—unconditionally, as your mothers could not—you will have made the most powerful choice of all.

I know I will see you again, wading into your precious life, knee-deep, hair swept back by wind.

You will turn. You will see me.

And this time, we will walk in together.

With hope and love

Yuk Lan

Letter Five - For Phoebe

This letter is for my granddaughter Phoebe, written during a holiday in 2020. It captures a fleeting, golden moment in our bond. She is the great-granddaughter of my birth mother, So Kam Lai—and she was one of the main reasons I returned to Hong Kong in search of my roots.

8th September 2020

Dear Phoebe

Part of me hesitates to write, afraid I won't do justice to the wonder that is you. Another part worries I'll sound too sentimental and people will mock. But I'll put all that to one side and I will write this as if I were reading it aloud to you in bed. In the big, soft bed in your special holiday room—the porthole room where Nai Nai, or sometimes daddy or mummy, would fall asleep curled around you after we'd read your bedtime story.

It's 5:00 am, and you're cuddling your pink dinosaur pillow, pressing your head firmly into mine and pushing me off my luxury white 800-thread-count rest. You're like a human alarm clock—with no snooze button. I love early mornings, but 5am is a stretch, even for me. Still, I know I'll miss this when you go home, that gaping 260 mile chasm suddenly reappearing to separate us.

You peel off the black paper circle we use to block the porthole window, letting in the dawn light. Like burglars in reverse mode, we creep out—through the door, past the safety gate—and pad to the living room that overlooks the harbour. Together we watch the sky break into bruised reds and magentas flecked with gold.

"Nai Nai, light candle," you say—not so much a request as a command. I light the tealight after our usual safety chat, and you blow it out with glee, transforming a mundane act into a small celebration. Ordinary Monday mornings are never ordinary with you.

You are extraordinary. Mischievous, curious, spontaneous. Perfectly imperfect and gloriously defiant. I want to rename the "terrible twos" something more worthy—something that honours your courage to stake your claim in the world. It's a miracle to witness: your thoughts bouncing like pinballs, your spirit uncontainable.

I know I'm meant to focus on your character, not your looks—but how can I resist? Your beauty glows from within, undiminished by snot or a lockdown fringe stuck to your forehead. You care nothing for appearances, and that's what makes you shine.

Phoebe, have we both inherited your great-grandmother So Kam Lai's spirit? Your Chinese family says Nai Nai is very much like her mother—someone who loved learning, enjoyed simple things, and had a head for business. I wonder if she too liked to wake with the sun and light a candle for the day ahead.

I hope you keep loving life's simple gifts. That you learn the greatest joy is to love and be loved in return. Don't be fooled by the idea that money or possessions equal happiness. I prefer time with family and friends to chasing city lights—and I hope you will too.

One day, you'll be able to read the story of how Nai Nai did once chase the city lights of Hong Kong. Went back to where she was born to find our Chinese family. And one day, we'll all go there together—me, you, daddy, mummy, and aunty Lucy.

The sun climbs higher as we scribble and paint. You swap the pencils and brushes between hands with ease, scatter sequins and googly eyes, while I try to calm my stress about mess and craft glue. You don't care. You are fully in the moment. You remind me that life is richer when we stop tidying the edges and let the spirit run free.

Now it's 6:38 am and we're building Duplo towers with your soft toys. I talk to your bears, and you talk back, so I don't feel silly. We sing

"Head, Shoulders, Knees and Toes (and Snotty Nose)," stretch out in baby yoga, and collapse giggling into "happy baby"—our feet pulled to our heads, rocking with laughter.

From that upside-down viewpoint, the world feels right again. Despite all that's broken—violence, illness, climate collapse, injustice—in this Monday morning moment, the world is made new. Because you are in it. Miraculous Phoebe, lighting up the world, one person at a time.

With all my love

Your Nai Nai

Letter Six -For Martin

Dear Martin
2017.
The future felt bright.
You had your contracts.
Long Lost Family had taken on my search.
For a moment it seemed
we both had what we wanted.
Then it cracked.
I pushed.
You withdrew.
We circled.
Patterns older than us both.
No villains.
No heroes.
Only two people
carrying what they did not choose.
There was love.
There was laughter.
There were years of making a life.
Love is not rescue.
It can be joy.
It can be grief.
It can be not enough.

L

Letter Seven - For My Birth Mother So Kam Lai

Dear So Kam Lai

As a child in the Heart of England, I dreamt of you. I was lost, but in my dreams, I found you. You cradled me in your lap, a whisper of green silk skirt wrapping around me as if I were a baby bird in your nest. You smiled down at me, and I knew you loved me.

Later, in a strange and foreign nest, I had to become a silent child about my memories of us—forbidden to speak your name, or ask about the one whose tenderness and touch I could only imagine. My adoptive parents didn't outright say, "Don't speak of her," but even as a small child, I instinctively knew not to.

Somewhere I read I was an intuitive and eager learner. That helped—I had a lot of catching up to do after a year in the orphanage, confined to my cot, amusing myself by playing with my elasticated name tag. The name you gave me: Tang Yuk Lan.

You gave me up—to the orphanage. Not abandoned on a doorstep. Not left without a name. I prefer to think of it like that. You gave me up—not gave up on me. Though sometimes I wonder—if I had been a boy, would you have fought harder to keep me? I don't blame you Mama. Everything you did was shaped by the time you lived in.

Once with my new English family, I began to walk and talk. Whatever Cantonese you may have spoken to me disappeared as I shifted into perfect English. Perfect, except I couldn't pronounce my brand-new name: Laura.

And underneath all those new skills, I learned something more fundamental, as if by osmosis: love and care in this new family depended on silence. On not speaking of you. On not asking where I came from.

Mama. Can you hear me trying to say mother in Mandarin? I tried to learn Chinese, just in case I ever got to meet you.

Mama—my adoptive parents have both died. My children are grown. I have more free time now. And I think often of all my parents. I wonder if there's an afterlife. And what it might be like.

Years ago, the television company Long Lost Family said they'd help me find you. They asked me to write you a letter. I tried—but what I wrote felt false and feeble. Instead, I wrote you a fable. For you, my birth mother—the woman I remembered from dreams. The one I could never speak of.

Now, with more of your story known to me—told to me by my sisters and brothers—I have rewritten that fable slightly. This is for you, So Kam Lai.

A fable for my birth mother, So Kam Lai.

Bring Her Home. The myth of the 100th birthday.

In the UK, reaching the age of 100 is cause for celebration. A letter from the Queen. A party with family—or whoever is still alive. If you're in a nursing home, maybe balloons, a banner, a cake, but never with 100 candles. A gift or two: Velcro-fastening slippers or an amplified mobile with a big red SOS button. The joys of reaching a century—over, but not quite out.

But what if you die before you reach 100? What celebration is left for you?

Everything in Hong Kong is different. My Chinese legend tells how it is even more revered to reach your 100th birthday in the afterlife. That is when Guan Yin, goddess of mercy, comes to find you in tian, or Chinese heaven. Guan Yin (觀音)—the mother who forgives all. The embodiment of compassion. She is called upon in times of despair, uncertainty, and fear. And on your 100th birthday, she grants you one wish.

Anything.

But if you die young, you wait. For a long time. Guan Yin does not rush. If you die at 99, though, you only have to blink—and she appears.

Some ghosts, silly things, still ask for Ferraris or lottery tickets, forgetting these hold no meaning in heaven.

You, So Kam Lai, died in 1997, aged 78. You waited 22 years—for 2019, the year your 100th birthday would be celebrated in the skies. And on that day, Guan Yin appeared.

This didn't surprise you. You had waited patiently, quietly certain. You knew your wish.

Before a wish can be spoken, the ritual must be honoured. You walked the long path to Guan Yin, hands cupped around a carved wooden bowl of water. You spilled not a drop. You poured the water into the lake of infinity. Circled Guan Yin's feet three times. Knelt. Pressed your forehead to the ground. Waited three long minutes. Then rose. Brought your hands to your heart. Pressed them together in prayer.

Only then did you speak.

"帶佢返屋企 (Daai kéui fāan nguk kéi)"

"Bring her home."

Cantonese makes no distinction between he and she, him and her—the meaning must be understood from context.

Guan Yin hesitated. "Your son?" she asked gently. She knew parts of your story. That you had ten children in total.

She thought perhaps you meant your firstborn son, who died in infancy during the Japanese occupation. Or your eldest daughter, also lost in that brutal time. Or the son who was sold away.

She wondered if you meant the twin boys you bore much later in life—your final attempt to give Mr Li a male heir. In the rural New Territories, traditional laws and customs favoured sons. Only a male child could inherit land or property. Even today, despite changes in legislation, certain long-held practices and policies continue to favour male descendants. No wonder, then, that so many baby girls were abandoned in post-Mao Hong Kong.

So many children. So much loss.

You shook your head gently. "No," you whispered. "Not my sons. My daughter. Tang Yuk Lan. Bring her home."

Letter Eight - From My Daughter Lucy Zanna to Me

After all this soul-searching and the many stops and starts to get this memoir finished, of course I hope it finds a wider audience than just my family and a few friends. But every time I let that hope rise, I find myself pulling it back down—still fearful of criticism and rejection.

Still, I know I must let go of those worries. Just as the search was for me and my family, this memoir is primarily for us.

Without my daughter Lucy—her curiosity about our heritage, her love of Hong Kong—I don't know if I would have kept searching. She visited Po Leung Kuk Orphanage in 2012, aged 19, when we were sponsoring a little girl. That visit left its mark. Unsurprisingly, she was the first person I allowed to read the draft of *Made in Hong Kong*.

While she was reading it, we spoke almost every day. At the same time, she was applying for a full bursary to retrain as an Integrative Arts Therapist. The morning she finished reading the memoir, she received news that she'd been awarded the scholarship. It felt like a sign—a symbol of how our journeys intertwine, how understanding our past can shape what's to come.

Her response to the memoir made every tantrum and tear worthwhile. I wasn't sure whether to include Lucy's letter—and if so, where it belonged. But after talking to her, we agreed: it had to be here, after my letter to So Kam Lai. My birth mother represents the past. Her granddaughter, Lucy, is the future.

Lucy writes to me:

Dear Mum

Here you are, across these pages, with your heart open, and your journey to Hong Kong perfectly documented. I read your blog during your search, as each entry was posted, but I still cried on the tube, in cafes, and in bed while rereading it all in your memoir. There are so many pain points expressed in ways I hadn't heard before—it's a strange experience to read a life I know so well, all packaged for a stranger to read. What a privilege to be allowed to read this before it reaches a publisher, in its rawest state—perfectly and imperfectly written before it's edited for wider consumption.

Here is this woman who took fate into her own hands, who, when she told me she was going to 'find her family in 90 days,' I didn't even bat an eyelid. Because the awareness that you have a choice, and then actively choosing, above all else, is the essence of you. Your spirit.

It is the joy you bring to life and the energy you exude—a spark that draws so many people. It's that spirit that says, '**** it, I'm going to live in a hostel for three months.' The driving force that makes it happen and allows it to happen. The attitude that goes, 'oh, I don't know how this is going to pan out,' but I'm going to try. You're like a little sprite.

You are the woman who picks herself up week after week and insists she will learn to roller skate at 62 despite others' forebodings, the woman who decided to learn the saxophone at 50 and now plays in bands. She, who runs away to the circus for the summer, rocks up in half a onesie with a bow in her hair and bright red lipstick, and does a little dance in the street when she feels happy. It's that part of you I found quite embarrassing when I was a kid but is now something I aspire to be. A bright, light, and carefree energy.

This is the essence that, perhaps despite the longing and the sadness and the wondering about the holes in your life, got you on that plane to Hong Kong.

It might be born out of hardship, it might not. It could be inherited—there might be a perseverance and resilience in the DNA we're all just starting to understand. There might not. I don't know what I believe, but whatever it is, wherever it comes from, it's the most special thing. It's the bit that connects all the dots.

I think we have all been searching; Tom, You, and I. Separately and together—through stories, language, holidays, and especially food. Trying to root our identities with what was available to us, without our Chinese lineage. Most recently, you have just guided me through attaining a diversity scholarship for a Diploma in Art Therapy. When I add in all our long talks about racial awareness, therapy, and education, it feels like something between us has come full circle.

I am so grateful you found our family. But I'm more grateful to have a mum who went out and tried. I love you.

Lucy

Unresolved

When I began writing this memoir,
I thought I was searching.
For origins. For a mother. For a home.

Instead, I kept circling myself.

A girl with a BOAC bag.
A blow-up Father Christmas with a hole in its head.
A white coat with pom-poms.
A girl whose arrival unsettled more than it soothed.
Who learned what it meant to be chosen,
and then unchosen.

The pattern showed itself slowly.
As a teenager, I left home after rejection.
As a woman, I left again —
a marriage, my children—for a time.
And now, at sixty-four,
I am once more in a room that is not my own.

It can look like running.
For years, I thought that's what it was.

But maybe stepping away
was the only way I knew
how to stay alive.

There is grief here.

Silence. Loss.
And also laughter.
Swimming.
Stubborn hope.

This is for those told to be grateful
when they are lost.
For those who leave
in order to live.

And to the infant with the chocolate-stained mouth.
The teenager who was not a tourist.
The woman with blue hyacinths.
The mother in a rented room:

you are still here.
You are telling it.

That is enough—

Acknowledgements

Thank you

- To my small and wonderful family—Lucy, Tom, Phoebe & Chloe. For being my little gems, my big rocks, and my total inspiration. I'm so blessed and proud to share approximately 10,000 centimorgans (cM) of DNA with you all.
- To Lisa—though we share no centimorgans, you are the best daughter-in-law. Thank you for always making me feel special, and for welcoming me so fully into your own small and wonderful family.
- To my mum, Cath Enock, and my dad, Arthur Enock—for all they taught me that I haven't written about here, including how to grow and cook good food on a budget, and a love for reading and being outdoors. They didn't always get it right, but they did their best. And without their choice to adopt me, I don't know where I would be.
- To everyone who read and commented on my original blog, told me I should write the book, and cheered me over the finish line.
- To my Cornish sisters, Anna, Ann and Paloma, who sent me off to Hong Kong with so much love, and welcomed me back, with more.
- To my dear friend Sheelagh, who always had my writing back through the thick and thin of this writing malarkey.
- To all my UKHAN fellow adoptees—your stories helped me shape my own.
- To Winnie—who gave me back my story, helped me claim my name and my family, and whose wisdom and love guided me home.

- To my 23 fellow Hoffman graduates and the Hoffman facilitators—without you, I would never have found the courage to forgive or reach any kind of resolution.
- And last, but not least, to Martin without whom this book would be different, or perhaps not at all.

Contact details

Contact
Laura Tan (Tang Yuk Lan)
✉@ Lauratan0@icloud.com

Printed in Dunstable, United Kingdom

67506329R00181